# GENTLE JOHNNY
# RAMENSKY

Also by Robert Jeffrey

*The Barlinnie Story*
*A Boxing Dynasty* (with Tommy Gilmour)
*Real Hard Cases* (with Les Brown)
*Crimes Past*
*Glasgow Crimefighter* (with Les Brown)
*Glasgow's Godfather*
*Gangs of Glasgow* (first published as *Gangland Glasgow*)
*Glasgow's Hard Men*
*Blood on the Streets*
*The Wee Book of Glasgow*
*The Wee Book of the Clyde*

\*

With Ian Watson

*Clydeside People and Places*
*The Herald Book of the Clyde*
*Doon the Watter*
*Images of Glasgow*
*Scotland's Sporting Heroes*

# GENTLE JOHNNY RAMENSKY

THE EXTRAORDINARY TRUE STORY OF
THE SAFE BLOWER WHO BECAME A WAR HERO

## ROBERT JEFFREY

BLACK & WHITE PUBLISHING

First published 2010
This edition first published 2011
by Black & White Publishing Ltd
29 Ocean Drive, Edinburgh EH6 6JL

3 5 7 9 10 8 6 4 2    11 12 13 14

ISBN: 978 1 84502 346 1

A CIP catalogue record for this book is available from the British Library.

Typeset by Iolaire Typesetting, Newtonmore
Printed and bound by CPI Group (UK) Ltd, Croydon, CR0 4YY

# CONTENTS

# ACKNOWLEDGEMENTS

A large number of people gave assistance in the production of this book. In particular I would like to acknowledge the help of the following people and organisations: The staff of the Glasgow Room in the Mitchell Library, the staff of the National Archives, Charlotte Square, Edinburgh, James Anderson, Johnnie Beattie, Les Brown, Dr Kathy Charles, Mrs E. Cook, Aileen Donald, Joe Dunion, Haig Ferguson, Kendal Ferguson, Charles Gordon, Mary Gordon, Harvey Grainger, John Hamilton, Elsie Ironside, Jim Ironside, Stuart Irvine, Peter Jappy, Dr Grant Jeffrey, Ed Johnston, William Johnston, Tommy Laing, Willie 'Sonny' Leitch, David Lovie, Dick Lynch, John Mathers, Jim McBeth *Daily Mail*, William McIntyre, Dorothy McNab, Mr X, Walter Norval, Liz Park, Peterman, Tam Purvey, John Quinn, Ronald Ross, Ed Russell, Tony Russell, Patrick Smith, Bob Smyth *Sunday Post*, Catherine Stevenson, Dorothy Thomson, Bert Watt, G. J. Wilson.

'Each man has an ambition and I have fulfilled mine long ago. I cherish my career as a safe blower. In childhood days my feet were planted on the crooked path and took firm root. To each one of us is allotted a niche and I have found mine. Strangely enough I am happy. For me the die is cast and there is no turning back.'

John Ramensky, Barlinnie Prison, 1951

# 1

# THE HARD LIFE

It was a hard childhood in a hard village – Glenboig in North Lanarkshire. And later in one of the toughest areas of a hard city – Glasgow's Gorbals. The saga of the life of the man who became famous as Gentle Johnny Ramensky began in the Lanarkshire of coal pits, clay mines, steelworks and brickworks in 1905, a time of conflict between immigrants from eastern Europe and native Scots, and ended two World Wars later in 1972. Between those dates, Johnny Ramensky led a life with the sort of highs and lows that are normally reserved for the movies.

Johnny Ramensky was undoubtedly a complex man. Part of him wanted a settled life, part of him wanted adventure, and he wrestled with these conflicting desires throughout his life. He was also well liked, as much by those in authority as those of the criminal classes. His chosen profession was safe blower and he was by far the most respected in his trade and the first name to be contacted if a criminal plan was being hatched that involved blowing open a safe. But his peacetime and wartime exploits also made him one of the most high-profile men in the land, a folk hero to many and a thorn in the flesh of authority. Being a criminal with a famous face plastered all over the newspapers is, however, not the most sensible way to keep out of jail, as Ramensky would find out. But it all contributed to the making of the man himself.

Despite its problems, there is no doubt that Johnny Ramensky relished his fame. After all, he was from a poor eastern European immigrant family, he had endured extreme poverty and he had made a name for himself against all the odds, even if it was a name not everyone would have wanted. He would have to endure years of incarceration for his crimes but, between these long stretches of time, were briefer interludes of adventure and excitement which really made him a household name. As well as becoming an astonishingly prolific jailbreaker whose latest exploits were avidly followed by the media, wartime service in the Commandos would set him apart from others and write his name into history as a legend, albeit a complex and highly flawed one.

The story of Johnny Ramensky begins with his early years in Glenboig, a time that shaped the boy and sowed the seeds of the man. He was born into poverty and deprivation and would later succumb to the easy money temptations of a criminal life – partially perhaps to ease his family's grinding poverty in the infamous Gorbals in the early years of the twentieth century. But he was also motivated by a deep and constant thirst for adventure. In his youth, he had a chip on his shoulder about his antecedents and suffered racial taunts in an era less politically correct than today. His family roots were in far-off eastern Europe and he was frequently teased and taunted as a 'Pole' though he was Lithuanian and a 'foreigner'.

During his life, Ramensky would acquire something of a Robin Hood tag which was frequently used by some of the more lurid tabloids but was perhaps not completely accurate. In the Glasgow of his time 'robbing hoods' were more of a speciality. But without a doubt he had some passing similarities to Robin of Sherwood. Johnny operated in the days when even among the toughest of the Glasgow slums there was something of a criminal code. Old ladies did not get bashed on the head for the meagre bags of shopping they were carting home from the local Co-op. Preferred targets for burglars and thieves were often businesses insured against loss, rather than private homes. And if a private home was the target it was more likely to belong to a businessman living in opulence in the suburbs than a struggling shipyard worker from a tenement close. He was, perhaps, a criminal of the old school.

Mind you, concentrating on 'tanning' businesses rather than homes is not completely daft. Many a villain would tell you that it is a sound notion to steal from the well insured – often you could go back and rob the same place again when it had reopened, by then tarted up and restocked with the aid of insurance money!

As well as the Robin Hood label there is a more exotic and slightly more realistic comparison in the Ramensky story – with that of the French felon Henri Charrière, played by Steve McQueen in the Hollywood film of his memoir *Papillon*. Glasgow historian and novelist John Burrowes included a chapter on Gentle Johnny in his *Great Glasgow Stories* (Mainstream, 2000) and headlined it 'The Peterhead Papillon'. Burrowes pointed out that Charrière, from the south of France, whose most sensational escape was from Île du Diable, the notorious penal colony off the coast of South America, was born within months of Johnny in the early years of the twentieth century. They both died aged sixty-seven, within months of each other. Each man made five jailbreaks and both constantly tried to record their adventures in prison notebooks. Charrière had more success with his scribblings than Johnny, however.

Papillon first saw the light of day in the pleasant sunshine of the Ardèche. Johnny was born in the less glamorous and less temperate surroundings of Glenboig. But in 1905 the Lanark-shire village at least had a commercial buzz and there was money-making going on in the place. Today it wears a resigned air of desolation, a village whose prosperity is visibly long gone. The air seems tainted with a whiff of better times past. Basically the village is now a crossroads, a pub and a post office and not too much else, though there is some little sign of life returning to the area with modern villas being built around the Farm Road area, in behind the pub, which is known as 'The Big Shop'. The reason behind the odd name for these licensed premises is simple and logical. As you might expect of such an area, there was in its heyday more than one pub. The smaller Glenboig pub, now closed, was known, with admirable Scottish working-class humour, as 'The Wee Shop'. Even the pub names tell a story.

Glenboig is not the sort of place you expect to find a 'Fox and Hounds', a 'Dog and Duck' or an 'Anglers' Rest'. Here Formica trumps wood panelling. Work, or perhaps in these difficult days in the twenty-first century 'no work', is the key. In the early days of Glenboig there was plenty of work. Hard work. Recreation then meant trying to beat the bookie or maybe making a name for oneself as a superstar of pitch and toss. At least you can still do that in the grim backlands of industrial Lanarkshire. And Glenboig has a claim to a place of honour in Scottish history as the birthplace of that extraordinary man Johnny Ramensky.

Work was plentiful in those days, but it was both hard and dangerous: mining clay and coal and making the quality bricks that were famous round the world. Fire clay brick manufacture began in Glenboig in the 1830s, largely as a result of the skills of the son of a Renfrewshire bleacher called James Dunnachie, who became the co-owner of the brickworks and was also involved in the mine. The bricks produced in this area by the Glenboig Union Fireclay Company and its successor, the Star Works, were soon judged 'to be superior to all others produced in Britain including the highly regarded Stourbridge and Newcastle bricks'. The quality was so high that orders were received from Russia, Canada, India and Australia and most European countries. Medals were won at building exhibitions in many parts of the world. These gold-ribbon bricks can still occasionally be spotted by the sharp-eyed in some of the now time-worn walls in the area. Often the bricks were emblazoned with large letters reading 'Glenboig' above a star, but even without a logo an expert can still identify them. Their fame was such that the makers of lesser-quality bricks used the local Post Office as a holding address in order that their letters carried the postmark

'Glenboig' and that allowed them to ride a little on the back of the success of the true Glenboig brick.

This was the birthplace of Yonus Ramanauckas, the man who was to become Johnny Ramensky, a.k.a. John Ramsay or Ramsey. This is where he spent his early years before travelling to the slums of the Gorbals with his family. This was the place that helped mould Johnny into the remarkable man he became.

I ventured into 'The Big Shop' one bitter snowy February afternoon, hoping to chat with any drinkers who had sought some warmth and refreshment in the bar. Surprisingly, and sadly, any youngsters around had barely heard of Johnny Ramensky, the village's most famous son. However, over a coffee, a local retired brick-worker called Joe Dunion, a small white-haired man, still fast on his feet, was able to tell me of seeing Johnny. This sighting had taken place in the very pub in which we were standing. On one of his brief respites from jail after the Second World War, Johnny had returned to Glenboig for a chat with friends from there or nearby Craigneuk, where many of the Lithuanian and Polish miners who came to Scotland had settled. Johnny, said Joe, was respectably and smartly dressed. In fact when you speak to relatives, fellow prisoners, policemen or acquaintances about Johnny, the first words they tend to use are 'respectably dressed' or 'smartly turned out'. Out of jail Johnny took great care over his appearance.

Joe Dunion remembers Johnny on his last visit to 'The Big Shop' as a figure given a lot of respect by old neighbours and fellow miners. To the drinkers at the bar that day, Johnny was an important and admired figure, already a legend. He drank little, but there was laughter in his company and many tales were being told of adventures as a cat burglar creeping across darkened city rooftops, or blowing safes behind the Nazi lines. Everyone was pointing him out and Joe Dunion remembers him looking 'European' amidst the Lanarkshire men.

Joe has a great interest in local history and he took me to the place where 11 Ashbank – the house where Johnny was born – is thought to have stood. The actual houses, miners' rows of the type you can still find occasionally in desolate odd spots in rural Lanarkshire, are no longer there. They have been replaced with a few bungalows and beyond, over a field or two towards Coatbridge, by a housing estate. Joe and I wandered a few hundred yards back down the road, where we stopped and looked over a farm gate and into a field beyond. This unremarkable steel farm gate gave no sign to the passer-by that it once led to the site of the famous mine where Johnny's father, Wincas Ramanauckas, had worked as a strike-breaking clay miner. Wincas, who had married Johnny's mother Mare (often known as Marie in Scotland) in Virbalia Miestely, Lithuania, in November 1897, was one of hundreds imported from eastern Europe to help drive the Lanarkshire men back to work during a stoppage.

The mine and factory owners in these rough days were indeed a ruthless breed. Scabbing is the worst offence in the trade union rulebook to this day and there is no doubt that there was considerable antagonism at the time between the incomers and the native Scots. Some of the hard feelings must have percolated, perhaps subconsciously, into the psyche of the young Ramanauckas, leaving scars of resentment that would surface years later.

As time wore on, the Poles and Lithuanians who came to Scotland to earn for their families were often spared the worst of the working-class hatred against strike-breakers as all miners, in their dangerous world, have a grudging respect for their fellows who toil underground, wherever they come from. But at the time there was much bad blood around. The Ramanauckas family must have struggled with the antagonism as they fought to make a new life and learn a new language, far from eastern Europe.

The sheer numbers of immigrants ensured that assimilation was a slow business. By 1914, it is estimated that 4,000 Lithuanians had settled in Lanarkshire. At that time, the distinction between Lithuanians and Poles was ignored by the Scots, who tended to call all the immigrants 'Poles' – which is more than a tad insensitive and a bit like referring to the Scots as English. A small point, perhaps, but nonetheless strange in Scotland, a country that takes so much pride in the difference between itself and its neighbour to the south.

More significant – and indicative of the state of conflict between the eastern Europeans and the Scots, whose jobs they threatened – is the fact that Keir Hardie, founding father of the Labour Party, helped lead a xenophobic campaign against the immigrants. Another factor in a dangerous mix was that the flood of incomers was largely composed of Jews and Catholics who had a way of life that was alien to staunch Scottish Protestants. It is said that most of the Jews settled in the Gorbals and most of the Catholics in Lanarkshire, where by 1905 there was already a Lithuanian priest in residence. Around that time there was also a Lithuanian social club and, a little later, even a newspaper – *Iseiviu Draugas* (the 'immigrant's friend').

Interestingly, at the time of maximum Polish immigration to Scotland, under EU legislation in the late twentieth and early twenty-first centuries, newsagents in some areas, even as far away from the industrial central belt as rural Kintyre, sold imported copies of Polish tabloids. But that was almost a century on.

Keir Hardie was far from alone in his opposition to the immigrants fleeing Europe for Scotland. John Wilson, Unionist candidate for St Rollox in Glasgow at the general election of 1900, did not believe it proper for 'this country to be the dumping ground for the paupers of Europe' and the trade unions and trades councils were opposed to the immigrants. It is interesting to speculate how much of this feeling of being an unwanted outsider in an, at times, unwelcoming land played in the forming of the Ramensky character. Maybe that was one reason for his desire to be something of a loner in his later life of crime, a man who was mostly a 'freelance' safecracker or a lone wolf rather than a criminal committed to one gang or one circle of law-breakers.

The various transmutations of the name Ramanauckas to Ramensky or Ramenski, or eventually Ramsay, are typical of what happened to the flood of workers from eastern Europe around the turn of the twentieth century. Immigration officials and pit bosses, often confused by complicated names they couldn't pronounce, labelled the workers at random. Like it or not, the new guys found themselves known as Willie Stewart or Jimmy Smith. It is said that one miner who signed a pay form with an X was thereafter Joseph Ecks.

Something similar seems to have happened to Johnny when he first went to primary school in Glenboig. The assumption is that the teachers found the proliferation of Lithuanian names confusing so, arbitrarily, Ramanauckas became Ramensky. Why the educational authorities did not simply rename him Ramsay or something similar from the start is a mystery. It would have saved Johnny much angst if they had done so. In his early years, the foreign-sounding name brought much hassle to a man who had breathed his first in Lanarkshire and who went on to fight bravely for the country where he was born. And to feel fiercely that he was a Scot.

After the initial aggressive backlash, the Lithuanians and others from eastern Europe gradually began to be accepted. The process gathered pace when the real reason why the new-comers were here was more widely known and understood – some were escaping conscription in the Russian army, others were Jews fleeing persecution, even more were ordinary decent folk simply desperate to get out of poverty and ready to go anywhere for a better life. John Burrowes, author of several excellent Glasgow histories, remarks that at the time when Wincas Ramanauckas fled Lithuania, the place was like Kosovo in the 1990s. (Incidentally, another Glasgow writer, Colin McFarlane, brackets Johnny in the fame game with fellow Gorbals man Alan Pinkerton, who was on the other side of the law.) His detective agency brought him into contact with Butch Cassidy and the Sundance Kid and the Jesse James gang. You can take the man out of the Gorbals . . .

Eventually the Scots' passion for fair play for the downtrodden began to kick in and over the years the newcomers from mainland Europe became accepted. Another factor in the process of assimilation was schooling. Johnny and his classmates must have learned a lot on both sides as the cultures merged.

Some of this was going through my mind as Joe Dunion and I leaned on that unremarkable iron gate and tried to imagine what the entrance to the mine had looked like in its heyday. On that oppressively dull, cold day, the shadows of the men who had trudged, a hundred years or so ago, down the sloping incline to the face where the clay was mined seemed to close in on us. This was not a pit, Joe explained; the difference being that you walk into a mine and travel down a shaft to a pit.

A few hundred yards from the old entrance to the mine, there is a pleasant little woodland walk meandering round a small lake. Even on that raw, snow-swept February day, mums with prams and kids, well wrapped up in scarves and knitted bonnets, took an afternoon constitutional round this reclaimed industrial land. Did any of them give a thought to the men who had laboured in daily danger, shovelling heavy spadefuls of clay, deep underground beneath the flower-edged paths of today to provide the raw material to make the famous Glenboig bricks? Somehow I doubt it.

It is not rocket science to work out why the site for the Glenboig clay mine was chosen. A thick, creamy sludge of greyish clay stuck to our shoes and ran in ugly little rivulets down the gutters of the steep street leading towards the centre of the village. And if you asked any gardeners among the nearby householders you got quick confirmation that this was the place to be if you were after top-quality clay rather than an earthy loam suitable for good gardening. Peat must sell well in garden centres near Glenboig. The attraction of the area's abundance of top-quality clay was such that the famous brickworks were built almost within yards of the clay mine entrance – raw material and final production process, side by side.

You could imagine you felt an oppressive air of sadness in the place. Perhaps it was because near here, where Joe and I stood, one of the most tragic episodes in Lanarkshire history was acted out. It happened on a calamitous day in August 1909. Johnny would have been a child of four at the time, but the proximity of his home to the mine and the dramatic scenes on his doorstep lead you to suspect that he would have been aware of the horror. Certainly his parents would have witnessed it, even if he himself was too young to see or appreciate the full appalling result of the tragedy. Wincas was employed in the mine. Although he escaped the disaster, one of the victims was Joseph Anderson, who lived in Ashbank, just a few doors away from the Ramanauckas family. They must have known the man well. The accident in the Glenboig Union Fireclay Company mine caused four deaths. A group of six miners had placed a shot (an explosive charge) at the face and retreated. The shot was fired normally and they made their way back into the working area. Then, without warning, a portion of the roof thought to weigh twenty tons fell on them. Luckily the debris missed two of the miners, but the other four were trapped under the clay and died a horrible death. It took an hour to reach them and bring the first body out.

Then followed a truly horrific scene. News of the fall had spread throughout the village and within minutes of it happening a large crowd, mainly women, had gathered at the mine entrance. As the bodies were carried out of the deep darkness of the mine into the August light, friends and relatives of the deceased cried out as the victims were laid on the bare earth. One little boy, recognising a body, cried out, 'Oh, that's ma faither!' and fled the scene in tears. Many of the women were in hysterics. James Donnachie, co-owner of the brickworks, who had been in Glasgow that afternoon, came immediately to the scene by car – an indication of his wealth. He expressed to the press his sadness and his concern that he could not understand the cause of the accident.

The shot fired was of the usual kind and the men had taken the normal precaution of examining the roof before re-entering the area. It was the only case of such a fatal accident to occur in that mine. Not for the first time, a mining village had suffered a grievous blow. It was a regular story – too regular – in mining communities the length and breadth of Britain in the days when health and safety at work was a distant dream. The lure of big money made many a mine or mill-owner take shortcuts, risking the lives of their employees. This time, tragedy had happened on the Ramensky doorstep and the family grieved, along with all those living in Glenboig at the time – especially those with family members who earned their living underground. They also learned all the better the dangers of working with explosives. Johnny faced those dangers all his life – as a miner, as a safe blower, as a Commando saboteur.

But there were a few happier memories for Johnny before 1913, when his father died and the family moved from Glenboig to a tough life in the Gorbals. Catherine Stevenson is a sprightly, outgoing and friendly pensioner, a retired social worker. She has a lively twinkle in her eye, and a good memory of what it was like for Lithuanians like the Ramanauckas family in the early years of the century in Lanarkshire. Now in her eighties, Catherine was born as Katarina Builbidus to Lithuanian parents living in Hamilton.

She got to know young Johnny well through family connections. Her father Yuzef was a baker who had turned to mining and had taken a tortuous route out of Lithuania through Romania and Germany to Scotland. It was a hard, sometimes dangerous, journey made by thousands. It is said that when they arrived in Leith, after a rough North Sea crossing, some of the immigrants thought they had arrived in America! Yuzef ended up making his way as a miner in Lanarkshire and it was not long before he sent home for a bride. Catherine's mother travelled to join him aged only twenty. Catherine says that now we would call it an arranged marriage. In those days it was not all that unusual. Yuzef was soon fluent in English, but Catherine's mother, who lived for fifty-five years in Lanarkshire, never spoke English. Again, this was quite common. Johnny's parents were also far from perfect English speakers though he himself became well spoken and articulate and learned to write English to good effect.

Catherine says the women in the Lithuanian communities in those days were so immersed in their own family lives, and the lives of their immigrant friends, that it was simply not necessary to speak fluent English – though they soon acquired the ability to get by with shopping and other everyday tasks. She paints a vivid picture of what was a distinctive and often, despite the difficulties of the times, a happy way of life. A new life in Lanarkshire with at least some money coming in and no threat from invading militias or secret police was much more desirable than an uncomfortable existence in the old homeland. Like all newcomers, the Lithuanians tended to stay together in what would now perhaps be called ghettoes, but that seems altogether too harsh a word for life in the Scottish mining communities. The men worked hard underground or in steel-works. The women worked hard at home.

Catherine told me: 'The house was well kept. You would not usually find a Lithuanian whose house was dirty. It would not be palatial but it would be clean. Lithuanians were always quite well dressed – not that we had the money, but we had the ability – mothers would make the children's clothes, for example.'

But there was time for play, too, at regular gatherings in halls in Craigneuk, in Bellshill and sometimes in Glasgow itself. There was a pattern to such regular social evenings. Catherine recalls: 'It was a meeting of people of similar backgrounds getting together. They would put food on the table, black bread – sweet and sour we call it now – and cold meats, tea and coffee. There would be a musician there with an accordion, who would play away in the background. The children would play among themselves, often crawling under the tables, and the adults sat and talked or danced to the tunes of the old country.'

The young Ramensky, his brothers and his sisters Agnes and Margaret would be at home on such evenings when the Lithuanians celebrated their independence and their identity, distinct from their Scots neighbours and fellow toilers in pit and factory. But for most of the time there was a striving by the Lithuanians to fit into their new homeland. Catherine says: 'We were always taught, because we were Lithuanian, people hadn't to see us as different. But we were always regarded – and don't think I am being facetious here – as cleaner than the other kids. Your mother made your clothes, a skirt and a top, and your hair was always in plaits and very often crossed over the top of your head. We did not have very much money, but one thing I will say about most Lithuanian women: they were very good house-wives; they could turn their hand to anything. I always tell my daughter, Katarina Adele, that when you went to a Lithuanian Mass all the people were smart and scrubbed clean and nobody was scruffy.'

Johnny had an aunt in Craigneuk who had dropped her Lithuanian name and settled for being known as Mrs Andrews. In those far-off days, holidays of any kind were a novelty, but on the basis that a change is as good as a rest, young children were often shuttled around family members. So it was that young Catherine used to travel the few miles from Hamilton to Craigneuk for a wee holiday with Mrs Andrews. Catherine says: 'Mrs Andrews had a daughter called Sylvia and she was the same age as me. She is still living in America.'

She also has vivid memories of the Ramanauckas family. 'I can remember Johnny's mother clear as yesterday. She was quite a wee, well-rounded, plump lady, who had only one arm. I didn't know how she had lost the other.' This was a disability that made housekeeping, dressmaking and similar tasks difficult for Johnny's mother. (The loss of the arm seems to have happened in the classic sort of mill accident, when a machine was thought to have stopped, but suddenly restarted and caught the clothing of a worker. Wire safety cages and such like were not in use at the time.) Catherine went on: "Though I remember Mrs Ramanauckas well I never remember anything of Johnny's father. His mother was always pleasant to me as a wee girl. John used to come occasionally. He was a very handsome youth. Very blond, quiet – he wasn't a rowdy young man. But of course he was a good bit older than Sylvia and myself.'

Johnny's father seems to have been a shadowy figure – or maybe he was just too often away at work down the pit. There are also suggestions that at times he was overfond of a dram. This was not a trait passed on to his son who, although he liked the company of the pub and club, never drank to excess and kept himself fit well into his fifties. Catherine Stevenson says that Johnny's mother seems to have been by far the strongest influence – and the fact that she was disabled strengthened the bond between Johnny and her and increased his feeling of responsibility for her. She says: 'Do you know what I think – there was never any question of his father. There were always a lot of men at the Lithuanian evening gatherings, but there was never a man there belonging to Johnny or his mother. I think that probably because her arm was completely away Johnny had responsibility for his mother.' Catherine accepts the theory that this urge to care for his mother may have been a factor in his early thieving, which began after the family moved from Glenboig to the Gorbals.

Johnny's father did play an important role in one aspect of his life – explosives. Wincas Ramanauckas had plenty of experience in the use of explosives to blow open seams of coal or clay. He had started in Lithuania with the dangerous 'black powder', which was used by shot-firers in mines and which, before the invention of the detonator cap and modern explosives, was extremely dangerous. But by the turn of the twentieth century, quarries, mines and safe blowers alike moved to using the various versions of explosives that were coming on the market after Alfred Nobel had concocted dynamite – gelignite being a modification of gelatine-dynamite containing a high percentage of nitroglycerine. As a youngster, Johnny must have learned from his father a respect for explosives, a respect he always showed both working underground and in safe blowing. Johnny's mastery of the black art of cracking a safe was such that, in later years, detectives arriving at the scene of a bank robbery would look at the safe and the general state of the premises, shrug their shoulders and remark, 'Johnny again'. His trademark was a neat job, using just enough 'gelly' to do the business, without blowing the whole place apart. In later life he became an expert in the different types of 'gelly', which could be rigged to direct an explosion upwards, downwards or sideways. He also was expert in the use of oxyacetylene equipment when necessary in opening a 'can' in search of cash.

The late Paddy Meehan, wrongly convicted of the murder of an Ayr pensioner in 1968, did a few safe jobs with Johnny and once remarked he was the sort of safe blower who wanted to tidy up afterwards. Not a normal trait found in Glasgow's petermen. Mind you, Johnny did make the odd mistake and Meehan got some laughs in the pub with his tale of going to open a safe in the company of the master cracksman and their shock when the target turned out to be nothing more exciting than a fridge.

Catherine Stevenson's memories of Mare Ramanauckas were a journey into the deep past of Johnny's family history. However she has some more modern memories of the master cracksman. After the Second World War, she met him by accident on a visit to the Barras, the world famous street market in the East End of Glasgow. They immediately fell into conversation about the old days and he mentioned how he missed the Lithuanian food of his youth. Catherine invited him home for the first of several visits to her Hamilton bungalow to share a bit of a feast with her and her husband. Johnny took along his second wife Lily – they were then known by then as Mr and Mrs Ramsay and living in the Gorbals.

For a Glenboig boy, the meal must have brought back emotional childhood memories. The menu was a million miles from the prison fare, or the army rations, that had sustained him for most of his years. The meal started with a traditional raw fish dish of which Catherine says the Scottish equivalent would be soused herring. Beetroot soup, too, was a favourite and there were plenty of spicy sausages and the cabbage so beloved of eastern Europeans. Cold ham was also on the menu. What Lily, a more conventional Glaswegian, thought of the food is not recorded.

The chat and patter flowed back and forwards between the old days in Glenboig and around Johnny's many subsequent adventures in the Commandos in the Second World War. Catherine's husband enjoyed these suburban evenings, too. The Stevensons had met when they both worked in the Philips factory in Hamilton, before she went into social work, and her husband had 'a great regard' for Lithuanians. Assimilation had largely been accomplished in the area. He was 'kindness itself', as the Scots say, to Catherine's mum, and the fact that his mother-in-law didn't speak English at all well did not seem a barrier to their friendship. He managed a word or two in her native tongue and was good about taking her to Lithuanian social evenings or to Lithuanian Mass, where he blended in well with the immigrant community.

Mr Stevenson and Johnny got on particularly well. Catherine remembers the safe blower telling her husband he 'had had enough of prison life and was going to change'. (Not long after this conversation he was back on the wrong side of the law. It was a familiar story!) But the Stevensons and the Ramsays had hours of entertaining conversation.

Catherine says: 'In our house Johnny was happy to talk to my husband. They would sit there and chat for ages. My husband was a clever businessman, but he enjoyed Johnny, who wasn't boastful – he was a quiet, inoffensive type of man.' Johnny's first wife Daisy McManus had died in the early 1930s and was never mentioned on these nights. But Catherine was not too sure that Johnny and Lily were perfectly matched. Maybe Johnny's notoriety was part of the attraction for Lily, but Catherine found her unremarkable and she did not fit into the Lithuanian loop – they came from different worlds. She had a higher opinion of Johnny: 'Though you knew what he had been, he was still quite a refined person.' She also comments that on his visits out to Hamilton he was always immaculately turned out.

Catherine Stevenson also says Johnny carried himself with the distinctive demeanour of many Lithuanian men who, in her view, had 'charm, but not commitment'. She remembers a time when she was walking her dog in the Cathkin Braes, a beauty spot in the Southside of Glasgow. Seeing a man in the distance, she said to a friend walking with her: 'There's a Lithuanian man.' She sensed a certain something about his style of dress, the way he carried himself. And she was right. Many who knew Johnny commented that, although he was always open and friendly, there was a certain air of the man apart about him, a certain difference. Maybe it was that lack of 'commitment' that Catherine had commented on. These days we might say that his Lithuanian genes sometimes shone through all his life.

Johnny was just eight when his father died in 1913, and this was significant in shaping the man he became. He had two brothers, but one died young and the other eventually settled in Canada. From then on, Johnny felt he had a lifelong responsibility for his mother and his sisters Agnes and Margaret. It seems that Wincas had never really got his health back after the horrors of his early life in Lithuania and his condition was exacerbated by the rigours of mining life in Lanarkshire which, commonly, was tough and short.

Soon afterwards, the family moved to Glasgow. The move to the big city was an important event in Johnny's life. There is no doubt that the remarkable character of Gentle Johnny Ramensky – and the shape of his life to come – was formed not only in his early years in Glenboig, but in the hard times in the Gorbals a decade or so into the twentieth century.

# 2

# FIRST STEPS ALONG
# THE CROOKED PATH

Life in the Glenboig of mines, brickworks, danger and poverty did not have much going for it for an immigrant miner from Lithuania. But at least a lively youngster born in Scotland could play in the surrounding fields, hear the birdsong and watch clouds and the sun cross the sky. These were invisible to the men, literally beneath his feet, who dug out clay and coal in a working life of permanent darkness. In the winter, a boy could lark around in fresh clean snow, in summer roam pastures and woods. It was no rural idyll, but it must have been more desirable to a wee boy in short trousers than life up a stinking tenement close in Glasgow's most infamous slum area, a desperate place with a name infamous worldwide.

Down the years hard men and gangsters in their hundreds have claimed that it was life in the slums that drove them to crime, and according to their stories they were the victims. There was undoubtedly some truth in this. By the time he was eleven, Johnny was a street criminal having his collar felt by the sturdy Glasgow cops. Many of these were big men who themselves had grown up in the clear air of the spray-lashed Western Isles, who ended their days patrolling the mean streets of Scotland's greatest city. In later years, Johnny was to write that the Gorbals urchins of his youth and his life in the slums were to blame for his life of crime. It was a bit of a facile analysis: it has to be acknowledged that the difficult surroundings of the old Gorbals also produced their fair share of honest hard toilers – and some bright youngsters who took to education well, made their way up in the world, even to high-earning jobs in the professions.

In those days, the police had no mobile phones or squad cars. The beat cop was a sort of tough guy in a blue uniform who often administered rough justice on his own. Husbands known to have 'duffed up' their wives would sometimes get a 'doing' from the local cop to convince them that they should treat women with respect. The local teenage criminals were more likely to get a clip on the ear or a boot up the backside than an appearance in juvenile court. In the case of young Johnny Ramensky, the fact that he was in regular contact with the law from his earliest days does not seem to have had much of a deterrent effect. In the rough and tumble of life in the Gorbals, the distinction between right and wrong was blurred, for kids, for adults and for the young men who ran with the infamous gangs of the period before the First World War. Survival was all. But, above all, the thing that Johnny seemed to have picked up during the daily struggle in the slums was a thirst for excitement.

The blast of a beat cop's whistle and the light thunder from the sandshoe-clad feet of youngsters dodging up closes to avoid the men they called the 'bluebottles' were all part of a game of real-life cops and robbers. Little shame or conscience was involved: that was the way it was on the streets. The taste for adventure and the lust for an adrenalin surge never left Johnny. He simply could not settle to a regular job. Even when his likeable person-ality led policemen or friends to offer him a job – as happened many times in his life – his only concern was whether or not there was any 'excitement' in it.

He spent these formative years in the Gorbals of blackened tenements, outside toilets, rat-infested back courts, mass un-employment and poverty. There is a current trend for Gorbals folk who have escaped from the miseries of what was a bona fide ghetto to look back on life there through rose-tinted spectacles. The friendly 'we were all in it together' nostalgia of life up a close, often portrayed in an autobiographical genre, is not a picture I recognise as a reality. Certainly not for the majority.

One homely touch in these far-off days in the Gorbals would be the barrels of salt herring, much desired by the district's thousands of immigrants: Jews, Lithuanians, Poles and the Irish. They were placed outside the front door on the pavement of almost every provision shop in the sombre gas-lit streets. (Incidentally, a few of these barrels of salt herring could still be seen outside Gorbals shops as late as the 1950s). But mostly life there in the old days was lived in a dark, rancid mixture of unsanitary housing, poverty and crime. So it is perhaps little surprise that Johnny swiftly became a law-breaker.

Sixty or so years later, one academic social commentator remarked, in an erudite analysis of the Gorbals slums, that what was remarkable was not the number of youngsters who took to crime, but the number who didn't. This thought was mirrored many years later when a Barlinnie governor got to read Johnny's own story of his life of crime and war heroics, which he wrote while inside, scrawling his memoirs in more than thirty notebooks. The governor described any potential book made up of Johnny's diaries as interesting, indeed, exciting. And he remarked: 'His description of his early days in Glasgow shows how it is almost inevitable that a youngster in his circumstances, and with his penchant for gambling, should drift into crime.' Maybe. But as noted previously some did escape the ghetto.

And the governor's observation was a kindly one. It seems that the young Ramensky had made his first contacts with the police even before he was a teenager. His drift into crime has some hallmarks similar to the life stories of other infamous Glasgow criminals. The odd brick through a shop window, even when still in short pants, and sweeties snatched from café counters led to the cops feeling his collar for the first time and the first of hundreds of appearances before the beaks. It was an introduction to a life of crime experienced by many a young Glasgow lad – especially those without a fatherly hand to guide them.

From the start, it seems, Johnny was not destined to be one of the youngsters who triumphed over the appalling conditions of their upbringing and went on to lead a socially useful life. His war service apart, that was not a description that fitted his destiny. He left school at fourteen to follow his father into mining, though it is clear that from an early age he was enjoying the excitements of cat burglary and safe breaking rather than the boring, muscle-punishing grind of hewing coal underground. The danger in shot-firing to bring tons of black gold crashing down from the seams – in front of which men crawled, spade in hand – did at least bring a touch of excitement. But such underground thrills were insignificant compared with those provided by a life of crime, even if creeping across tenement roofs in the dark usually led to long periods swinging sixteen-pound hammers to break stones in prison quarries, and years of boredom behind bars, existing on the meagre prison rations of the early twentieth century.

As with many of his contemporaries, Johnny's drift into petty crime led to him tasting life in a borstal. He was sent to the famous penal establishment for young tearaways in Polmont in 1921. Borstal, called after a village near Chatham in Kent, was the name given to a system intended to rehabilitate offenders aged between sixteen and twenty-one. It dated back to 1902. It may or may not have worked for tearaway Londoners sent packing to cool off in the green rolling fields of Kent. But in the industrial city of Glasgow, to be known as an ex-borstal boy was almost a badge of honour on the streets. Central to the borstal ethos was the idea that it was better to deal with unruly teen-agers in a special institution rather than bang them up with hardened cons in an adult jail, where they would pick up lessons on the criminal life from the old lags. In theory, the separation was a good idea and life in borstal was no easy touch. It was a hard regime that included solitary confinement as a punishment, in an infamous underground cell known as 'the digger'.

The Polmont institution, in particular, had something of a reputation for brutality against inmates. Sometimes the boys were left by warders to sort out disputes with their fists in irregular boxing matches. The inmates may have been tearaways without much experience of criminal life and not really able to tutor each other in criminal ways, but the institution had one huge disadvantage in the business of redemption – the prestige its 'old boys' gained from surviving it and being released to thieve and fight again!

In some ways, borstal helped the young Ramensky in his chosen career, and as crime was his choice, he frequently turned down well-meaning offers of help to go straight. To the very end, this man would eloquently explain that his way of life brought him no regrets. He would do the same again given a choice.

The borstal regime suited Johnny. A small man at five foot six, he used his time in the gym to hone his inherent gymnastic skills. He also developed the astonishing upper-body strength that he used to great effect in clambering over rooftops in search of safes to break. His almost circus acrobatic skills were also to help in future escapes from jail.

He was released from borstal in 1924, but it was not long before he was in a real adult jail.

# 3

# JAILBIRD JOHNNY

Johnny Ramensky had been in serious conflict with the law since he was eleven, but the severity of the offences and the sentences grew from 1925 onwards. In that year, he pled guilty to sixteen charges of housebreaking and was given eighteen months. These crimes had been committed in many areas of Glasgow including Hyndland, Anniesland, Shawlands and Crosshill.

He was finally caught when one housekeeper returned unexpectedly and this incident led to a rare charge of assault being made against him. He was charged with compressing the housekeeper's throat, though it was said at the trial that the action 'was not of a serious character'. In pleas on his behalf the court heard he had used the Post Office to return stolen War Savings Certificates to their owners. The judge said he was reluctant to pass a heavy sentence on such a young man and that he would give him one last chance, despite his previous record. Johnny was warned that if he turned up in court again he could expect a hard sentence. It was not a warning he took to heart.

Johnny Ramensky was not a man who took a telling. He may at times have moaned about his treatment by the law, but the inescapable fact is that he was given more 'last chances' than his record deserved. During his extensive life of crime, he would be sentenced to around sixty years in jail and, taking remission on his various jail terms into account, he served more than forty years behind bars. If he had been allowed to, or encouraged to, he could have written a unique history of the evolution of prisons in Scotland in the twentieth century. He did time in them all: Polmont borstal, Saughton, Barlinnie, Perth, Craiginches. He was shackled in chains in Peterhead, and spent three years breaking stones in the quarries there, watched by armed guards. Then there were five escapes. Campaigns against bad prison food. Campaigns for fellow prisoners allegedly denied sufficiently speedy medical treatment. It would have been some tale. But, as we shall see later he ran into opposition to keeping diaries or writing his own story.

With his borstal days behind him, Johnny soon found that life in jail was very different. As his parents had been in Glenboig, Johnny was mocked as a 'Pole' and a 'foreigner'. Like most Scots of the time, his fellow inmates did not seem able to differentiate between Lithuanian and Polish descent, and their attitude seems to have eaten hard into his soul during his lonely hours behind bars. In Barlinnie he regularly moaned that the other prisoners abused him verbally because of his name and background and were prejudiced against him.

For most of his life in prison he conformed to the old lag's philosophy: if you do the crime you do the time and when inside you keep your head down and get on with it. He was not into attacking warders or trashing cells or prison canteens. But in his early days in prison, he was at times his own worst enemy.

In prisons, the conditions naturally lead to cons having feuds with each other and taking against certain prison warders. Fistfights can break out suddenly and dangerously. Considering the length of time Johnny spent locked up, he was involved in remarkably few spats of that nature. But he was not always the perfect prisoner. Throughout his prison years he frequently wrote letters to the authorities about his treatment. And he would take up pencil and paper on behalf of any fellow con he felt was not getting a fair deal. Interestingly for a man who left school at fourteen, he had a lifelong ability to write grammatically and coherently on his prison experiences.

Reading his letters on various complaints, held in the National Archives, a picture is painted of a restless, unhappy man always seeking the much-desired accolade of the long-time criminal – 'respect'. He often uses that clichéd emotive word in the ragged, ink-stained notes (blotting paper seemed to have been in short supply in HM Prisons sixty years ago!) either torn from cheap notebooks or written on official prison notepaper. His letters are inconsistent in their demands: at one time he wants a move from Saughton to Barlinnie, at others times he wants to be moved back from Glasgow to Edinburgh.

In November 1926, he wrote a letter to the governor of Saughton that underlines his love for his mother. Prisoner 1541 wrote:

> I am writing to you this letter so that you know the nature of my request. It is this. I would be very grateful if you would send me back to Glasgow. I belong to Glasgow and my parents, that is my mother and sister (sic), father being dead 14 years, could not afford to come through to Edinburgh to see me. I was sent from Duke Street to the High Court to be sentenced and am now detained in Saughton. My sentence is 18 months and the expense is too much for my people.

With this plea was a little note from the head warder, who said: 'John Ramensky is an ex-borstal inmate. Since admission to his present sentence his conduct and industry has been good.' It worked and soon he was back in the Bar-L. But a couple of years later he was pretty unhappy with life when again banged up in the 'Big Hoose' in Glasgow's East End.

A year earlier, he had written to the Prison Commissioners. This was a much more raw, emotional piece of writing, giving real insight into the mind of this complex man. These days, it would probably result in a session with a psychiatrist or a chaplain. It was treated more harshly then. He wrote:

Pardon me the liberty of writing to you but I would not do so unless I was forced. I am in great trouble here and write to you for relief. My name is John Ramensky and my sentence is 18 months. You will doubtless remember me writing to you before and so must apologise for causing you this trouble. Well, sir, please help me and I will never forget you. Little did I think I was to suffer? Everybody here in Glasgow seems to know me and take a dislike to me and delight in teasing me. They all know my name and I am a foreigner or as they say I am a Pole and looked down upon. I can stand it no longer and am writing to you to help me before I go mad. My life is a perfect misery and my nerves are bordering on the verge of insanity. In Saughton I was treated with respect and my work was appreciated and I was counted as a man. Send me back to Saughton. I have still 17 months to serve and three months remission to earn. In Saughton I was treated with respect and nobody ever asked me how long I was doing or your name and when refusing to tell them some other kind person who knew would oblige him and then I would be made fun of and called a foreigner and other such names, which will drive me so as I will not be responsible for my actions one of these days. I have always had good conduct in prison and would like to continue. So, sir, send me to Duke Street and whenever anyone is going to Edinburgh High Court they can take me with him or her to Saughton. I will gladly pay all the travelling expenses and if you would send me the bill I would see that it is paid. I prefer Edinburgh to any other place, as there the men are men and treat me as one of themselves. I am sorry for causing all this trouble and must apologise but you see how necessary this is. This to you means nothing but to me it is everything. So pity me before I go raving mad. So help me God. So grant me this appeal. Prison is bad enough, but spare me the madhouse. It means nothing to you and will cost you nothing.

The offer to pay the costs involved in this transfer shows a curious sense of integrity coming from a convicted criminal, though perhaps it was just a ploy to underline how desperate he was for a move.

The top man in Barlinnie at that time was Governor R. Walkinshaw, considered a fairly benign ruler of the establishment then. However, on perusal of Johnny's plea he did not call in the psychiatrists or therapists but merely remarked in a note that, 'I have heard nothing and learned nothing to support the prisoner's statements of being teased by others. His name discloses his extraction but I have not experienced any case of annoyance because of nationality for a long time.'

So much for Johnny's claim of being on the verge of insanity and in fear of the madhouse. In a handwritten note, the governor declared there was no reason for a transfer. He ended coldly by telling the warders to 'Inform the prisoner'. Attached to the documents was the final piece of paperwork on this issue, written by a warder. It simply said: 'Prisoner informed'. Inside the old-fashioned oval rubber stamp on the fading paper you can still read the date – 24 December 1925. Happy Christmas Johnny Ramensky.

Heaven knows Christmas is a sad, surreal time inside a prison at any time. Prisoners long for and remember family Christmases. That December must have been a particular hell for Johnny as his emotional plea was so curtly dismissed. It was hard in jail eighty odd years ago.

All this anguish and unhappiness was unknown to the general public but they were already beginning to follow Johnny's career in the newspapers. As he had noted in one of his letters, 'everybody here in Glasgow seems to know me'. That notoriety was heightened a couple of years later, on 26 July 1931.

These days, TV viewers and newspaper readers are fairly relaxed about rooftop protests in prisons. They surprise no one. Indeed one famous Scottish criminal was known as The Pigeon because he spent so much time roosting on the jail rooftops. The 'incident' – as the prison authorities liked to call it – in Barlinnie in January 1987 is well remembered. It followed similar riots in Saughton and Peterhead in the dying days of 1986. At Barlinnie, a group of prisoners, who had broken out of their cells and gathered high on the rooftops in the freezing cold, were involved the longest prison siege in Scottish history. There was a massive press corps a few hundred yards from the prison gates and TV and radio recorded every development. Few in Glasgow at the time will forget the remarkable images of wild men in balaclavas standing, hands outstretched, on the prison chimney tops demanding justice for prisoners they alleged had been treated badly. The whole circus lasted five days before the last of the protestors was coaxed down and back into the prison for pie and chips. Very Glasgow!

That was the second major riot in the prison. In the mid-1930s there had been a serious outbreak of violence in which warders and inmates clashed and there were many injuries. This had started over a dispute about smoking by unconvicted prisoners in the sight of those who were now serving their time and were not allowed the solace of tobacco. It was a classic example of how, when hundreds of men are caged together, a simple dispute can spread like wildfire from one cellblock to another. It shows how an easily solvable dispute can lead to a major incident. Those with a knowledge of Scottish penal history call this incident 'the tobacco riots'.

Less well known is that in the summer of 1931 there had been a mad 'circus' on a Barlinnie rooftop, in some way similar to the shenanigans on the roof in the 1980s. But this time it was a one-man show starring Johnny Ramensky.

On 31 July of that year, at around two in the afternoon, he was exercising in the yard of E-Hall when, without warning, he suddenly tore off his boots and in stockinged soles raced across to a rone pipe in the corner of the yard. He climbed up seventy feet almost effortlessly and ended up high on the roof. It had all happened so fast that the startled warders could not reach him in time to catch him or impede his upwards progress. Their first efforts to get him down ended in farce. The warders dragged out fire hoses intending to wash him off the roof, but the water pressure was so low the jet could not get anywhere near him. In any case the hose, unused for years, leaked and it was warders, rather than the prisoner, who were cooled off by the spray from the perished rubber. From his rooftop perch, Johnny was tossing down slates hoping the sharp edges would deter the warders from pursuing him and also maybe further puncture the hose to wreck this attempt to wash him down.

There was no live TV and radio in those days to attract a crowd outside the prison walls to watch the fun. But Barlinnie, a huge imposing structure, always had a few gawpers looking at it as they passed along the neighbouring streets. The word soon got around that there was a show worth watching at the jail. Newspaper reports of the time say that, astonishingly, almost 4,000 people watched the antics on the roof from Lethamhill Road and surrounding fields. Johnny did not let his audience down. He paraded along the highest point of the roof with 'the skill of a circus tightrope walker' and when finished with that he stood on the edge of the roof doing improvised dumbbell exercises and 'physical jerks'. He even stood balanced on one foot for a spell. In between times he shouted down for the warders to throw him up a boiled egg or two. Obviously he was indulging in his famous sense of humour so often commented on by people who knew him. He also told the warders that they had not allowed him to join the work parties within the prison walls – who at least got an hour or two of fresh air – but that he was outside now. It was a remarkable pre-planned performance. The master cat burglar and rooftop runner gave those inside and outside the prison a show to remember.

This bid for glory, at least inside the Bar-L, came about, he later told friends, because of a desire to be a bit of a hero to the other inmates. A bid for that old balm for the criminal ego, respect. It seems all those smears of being 'a Pole and a foreigner' had festered inside his mind and finally pushed him into action. How were the authorities to handle this one?

Prison chaplains are remarkable people who have to look after their flock inside – and their families – while maintaining a good relationship with the staff. Often the chaplain knows more about what is going on in the prison than anyone else. And often when there is trouble they roll up their sleeves and help to sort it out. The man in the dog collar in Barlinnie at the time of Johnny's rooftop exploits, the Rev J. McCormack Campbell, was typical. Many years later, he still remembered the drama and farce of the prisoner on the roof and the abortive attempts to hose him down. He told Edward McCartney, a legendary reporter on the old Glasgow *Evening Times*, that this was Johnny showing his daredevil streak long before he joined the Commandos.

Barlinnie has one place where it is possible to sit in the presence of your own god, if you have one, and feel for an hour or so that you are on the outside while still inside, as it were. This is the prison kirk, a place of quiet – designed like a turn-of-the-century suburban church. It is one of the most remarkable structures in the daunting grimness of Barlinnie; a building like no other in this oppressive, forbidding complex. The story of the chaplain's first encounter with Ramensky began in the calm of this unique place of worship. He told it like this:

Inside the prison church hall that lovely summer Sunday afternoon I was conducting the usual after-dinner service when the prison alarm bell went. I decided to carry on as if nothing had happened. Outside we could hear hustle and activity. I tried to appear as unconcerned as I could. So, to their credit, did many of the prisoners. The service over, I found Ramensky on the roof. All attempts at recapture were being met with showers of slates and other missiles. An hour went by and I climbed the stairs leading to the roof and pleaded with him to surrender. He listened for a time then he made up his mind. If I didn't get back down the slates would come at me.

Outside the walls, crowds were gathering quickly to watch Ramensky dodging behind a chimney head then reappearing to fire another charge of slates.

Some hours passed and eventually the governor, who had been away from the prison, returned. He sent for a prisoner called Tom Clark – described as Ramensky's special chum in official reports. Clark was sent up a ladder to speak to the nonchalant man on the roof and try to talk him down. At Clark's heels stood a warder called Hugh McDowall who was told, 'to go to the ladder and listen to the conversation between Ramensky and Clark'.

McDowall reported: 'Prisoner Clark began by asking, "How long do you intend staying up there, John?" Prisoner Ramensky said, "I am out for an airing and may stay a day or two till fetched." Clark then said, "Come away man, don't be silly, no one will hurt you." Ramensky replied that they had better not. Prisoner Clark then said, "What caused you to do this?" and Ramensky replied, "I asked the governor to let me out to the stone yard and he could not see his way to do so. I have just gone up to get some fresh air." Clark then asked if he would speak to the governor and he said he would.'

The governor then apparently went up the ladder and persuaded the prisoner to come down, which he did via a skylight. He had been on the roof for five hours and at the end all you could see were a few missing slates and the odd crust of bread that Johnny had saved from breakfast and lunch to ward off the pangs of hunger during his rooftop 'act'.

The chaplain did not put Johnny's eventual return to the prison down to the assurances that the warders would not harm him. No, he told old 'Ned' McCartney that up there on the rooftop the escapologist said to the governor: 'I am glad you came, I am hungry!'

Even Governor Walkinshaw noted in a report on the incident that this was a bid for respect. Johnny wanted to be 'a big man, a hero to the others'. In this he obviously succeeded. With the papers reporting his antics at length, much to the amusement of their readers, he burnished his own legend as a character. Johnny never ran into career guidance at school, but this episode seems to suggest that maybe he should have taken that age-old escape from a troubled young life and run away to the circus. His head for heights, his delight in putting on a show, and above all his strength and agility would have made him a star on the right side of the law!

The reference to his desire to work in the open air in the stone yard and the governor's refusal to let him do so is interesting in view of Johnny's legendary non-violent status. Barlinnie had at that time all sorts of workshops, making everything from fenders for ships to mats and furniture. The reason Johnny had been banned from the stone yard – where prisoners broke rocks wearing improvised gauze masks to protect their eyes – was that he had been involved in a fight in the mat-making workshop. It is easy to imagine, though, that this was as a result of him being taunted as to his ancestry and fighting back.

Clearly Johnny was fighting fit during this escapade on the roof. He had the prison authorities to thank for that. He could have died unknown to the public in Barlinnie. Indeed prompt action by the authorities had saved his life. He had contracted pneumonia in the summer of 1930 and the prison doctor wrote: 'The disease threatens immediate danger to life and can not be treated in prison.'

He was taken to the nearby Lightburn Hospital in the East End and the medics there did a good job with him. A month later he was returned to the jail 'looking well: chest apparently cured'.

This experience was in stark contrast to what happened to some of Johnny's fellow inmates in Peterhead decades later. According to Johnny, they did not get such prompt life-saving treatment. It was a claim that put him in a long-running dispute with the Peterhead authorities. It is also interesting that when in

Lightburn he made no move to escape despite the fact that he was on home turf and near family and friends – perhaps there was no challenge in getting out of such an establishment. Or maybe he was just too ill, or grateful to the folk who had saved his life. Not to take a chance to escape was not like him.

# 4

# HUNTED DOWN

Throughout his life Johnny Ramensky was philosophical about doing the time if he'd done the crime. Which, given the number of crimes he committed and the jail time he got, was just as well. However, Ramensky wasn't always happy to stay locked up. Part of the game for him was the fact that he could escape from pretty much any prison he chose to, high security or not. And his frequent and high-profile escapes became a key part of the Ramensky legend.

If the stay in Glasgow's Lightburn Hospital was a missed chance to flee from incarceration to the dangerous excitements of freedom on the run, it was not typical. So adept was Gentle Johnny at scaling prison walls that at one stage in his career it was remarked, only half-jokingly, that at times the staff at Peterhead did not know if he was in or out!

Scotland's most northerly major jail was built in 1888 near the North Sea, thirty-two miles north of Aberdeen. The bald record of Johnny Ramensky's escapes from this grim place only hint at a series of remarkable adventures. He escaped the grim fortress in the north-east five times in all – in November 1934, August 1952, and three times in 1958, in January, October and December. All his life he craved drama, tension, suspense and thrills. Sometimes he got them from gambling away large wads of cash; sometimes they came from breaking the law. Sometimes they came from breaking out of prisons.

His first escape from Peterhead in the winter of 1934 did not make headlines quite as large and lurid as those used by the tabloids today. Newspaper layouts in those days were much more sedate, with the births, marriages and deaths on the front page. But this was big news nonetheless and after his rooftop antics at Barlinnie the public was beginning to develop a voyeuristic interest in the activities of Gentle Johnny. The legend was starting to feed on itself, as legends do, and the events in Aberdeenshire more than seventy years ago were a potent factor.

Getting out of Peterhead was no easy matter, with the North Sea on one side and the exposed moorland of Buchan on the other. Ramensky's first escape was a classic – worthy of a film on its own! And it happened in the gripping cold of a northern November. The details show just how tough Ramensky was, a toughness that would serve him well in foreign fields. There are few facts on how this classic escape was actually carried out but the newspapers of the time were certainly accurate when they described Johnny as a man of great physical strength and cunning.

Willie Leitch is a legendary figure in Scottish prison history and a man who shared friendship and prison time with Johnny. He once showed me how he believed Johnny could scale walls without the grappling irons or ropes used by lesser men. He believed that Johnny was strong enough to stand with his back against a sandstone corner wall and, with his shoulders wedged between the two sides, slowly heave himself up the wall. No wonder Johnny built up a reputation for circus-style gymnastics.

Willie gave me his demonstration in a popular Lanarkshire howff and the customers must have wondered what on earth was going on! Willie is one of the few prison contemporaries of Johnny still living. He is widely known as 'Sonny' – this nickname came from an incident when as a boy he and his pals found a wartime bomb crater in the road. Willie jumped into it, perhaps in search of shrapnel, something the war kids liked to collect. Along came a local aristo who stopped his Roller at the crater, leaned out and asked, 'Sonny what are you doing down there?' Willie's pals collapsed in laughter at this and the name stuck.

A lively guy with a sense of humour, Willie is a touch on the plump side, though still, despite his age, a fan of fast cars and no mean driver. These days he has no need of getaway cars! His main concern now is trying to get justice for his Royal Navy colleagues from the Korean War, who he thinks did not get a fair share of medals for their bravery. When not e-mailing Navy top brass and Westminster politicians about his campaign, he loves to talk about the man who was to him something of a hero, Johnny Ramensky.

Notwithstanding Willie's eye-catching demonstrations in a pub of how to climb a prison wall, Johnny was, of course, not slow to use a ladder if he could find one handy while escaping. But his head for heights and his climbing skills would have fitted easily into any world-class rock climbing party. And it should be remembered that even the highest of old prison walls were constructed in a way that left narrow ledges and tiny crevices to be exploited by a daring and strong climber. Today most modern prisons have smooth perimeter walls topped with barbed wire, which makes getting up and over them a much more difficult task.

Incidentally Willie Leitch himself, who turns up again later in this story, used more cerebral than physical methods in his own escapes. He was also known as the 'Saughton Harrier', a sobriquet derived from a daring and devious escape from the Edinburgh jail. When languishing inside, he read in the papers of a marathon run due to pass the prison in a day or two. Wily Willie secretly manufactured a runner's vest complete with number and got himself a pair of trainers. On the day of the marathon Willie was working, tending the roses in the governor's garden. When the main pack in the marathon passed the garden, Willie slipped over a wall and joined them. Looking the part in his athletic rig, he simply disappeared, striding powerfully into the invisibility of hundreds of similarly dressed runners.

Willie managed to stay free longer than Johnny, who usually only managed a few days out of jail and never got very far from Peterhead before recapture. Willie Leitch managed almost six months on the run. Interestingly, many who knew Johnny think that one of the reasons he never travelled far from the jail in any of his escapes was that he did not really have much desire to stay on the outside as a fugitive. Getting out was the challenge he relished, not staying out.

Johnny's 1934 escape from Peterhead was, however, a more rugged affair than the exploits of the Saughton Harrier. It was the first escape from a prison that some observers bracketed with Alcatraz and Dartmoor as secure fortresses. A couple of years earlier a prisoner had escaped from a work group in the Peterhead quarry, but he had died under rifle fire from the warders. Johnny was the first man to get outside from the inside, as it were. He was up and over the walls between six and seven in the morning, without even a good pair of boots to help over frosty fields and roads. The weather was vile, with regular snowstorms. He was dressed in a prison suit of brown moleskin with long trousers and a battle-dress type of jacket and he had on black shoes but no headgear of any kind.

The alarm signalling his escape sparked massive police activity. Farms were searched, road junctions watched and hundreds interviewed in the hunt for the escaper. But he still managed to reach Ellon. This was the scene of one of the most remarkable feats in his career. The bridge over the Ythen was blocked at both ends by police vehicles and a posse of officers. Within earshot of them, Johnny managed to cross the bridge, swinging hand-over-hand underneath the road from girders and projecting stonework. On the other side, away from sight or sound of the police search parties, he hid in the loft of a garage until darkness, which at that time of year in northern Scotland comes early, bringing with it a biting coldness.

Hours later, he swam across the near-frozen waters of the River Isla, a tributary of the Ythen. He was finally traced to Foveran where he had been spotted in a field. The police gave chase across open ground. Eventually the escaping convict was brought to ground like a hunted animal, exhausted and weakened by exposure and more than two days without food. He showed no fight, even though he had an iron bar in his hand. It is said that he even joked with his captors.

This was a typical Ramensky arrest – resisting the cops when caught was never Johnny's style. He had been free for twenty-eight hours. One theory on how he made this escape underlined Willie Leitch's account of Johnny's gymnastic ability, strength and courage. The suggestion is that he clung to a ledge in the prison wall using his hands alone for half an hour; then when he judged the coast was clear he finally swung himself up and over the top of the wall. Some feat.

On his return to prison, Johnny made some more history. The authorities ordered that he should be shackled. Although his feet were swollen from his time on the run, leather anklets were put on his feet and steel rings were welded in place on top of them. The rings were joined together by a heavy chain, which was gathered up and fastened to a thick leather belt around his waist. This indignity and cruelty left him barely able to shuffle around his cell; a pathetic sight. To enable him to change his clothing, his trousers and underpants were split from top to bottom at the seams. It was, as he remarked in later interviews, as if he was being forced in the most cruel possible way to learn the hard lesson that he must not break into – or out of – places.

The newspapers reported in depth this barbarous treatment of a man who was, even in the 1930s, well known to the public; a man who had a large measure of respect for his non-violent attitude. The stushie filled the pages of both broadsheets and tabloids, angering their readers – and it went all the way to the House of Commons. John McGovern, the Independent Labour Party MP, asked the Secretary of State for Scotland if his attention had been drawn to the form of punishment being meted out to Johnny when in solitary.

Then, as now, bad publicity can move political mountains. A few days after Westminster got involved, a blacksmith suddenly appeared at Johnny's cell door with hacksaw in hand and in December 1934 the inhumane torture of the shackles was ended. And not just for Johnny – never again was a prisoner in a Scottish jail subjected to such callous treatment. Johnny may not always have appreciated the headline-grabbing tendencies of his antics but in this case his infamy worked in his favour. And that of everyone held in prisons in Britain. It was a monumental episode in his career.

That Johnny was in Peterhead in November 1934 was largely the result of the detective skills of one man. And that man was later to become a friend of Johnny over the years and play a major role in the ongoing saga of the remarkable safecracker. He was Superintendent John Westland of the Aberdeen CID. Westland had first met Ramensky in March of that year in Perth. Early in the morning of 25 March, a major robbery had been discovered at the head office of well-known bakers, Ledingham's, in Mount Street, Aberdeen. As usually happened, Johnny's skill in blowing the safe played a part in his downfall.

On this occasion the detectives in Aberdeen, though not as familiar with his work as their colleagues a few hundred miles away in Glasgow, could not help but see that the robbery was the work of a master in the art of safe blowing. This was clearly the work of a skilled criminal, not that of the usual thieves in the area or of someone just learning the skills of the peterman. This was a classy job. The Aberdeen cops got an early lead when they heard from colleagues down in Glasgow that it was rumoured among the criminal classes on the streets of that city that Johnny had been planning a wee trip out to the country. And not for a holiday.

Westland acted quickly by calling the CID in Perth, which was on the rail line from Aberdeen, to make sure the boys in blue were there in Perth Station to meet the morning train from Aberdeen to Glasgow as it steamed and clanked its smoky, noisy way south. The carriages were duly searched in meticulous fashion and Johnny and a companion, his brother-in-law Mario de Marco, were found on the train. Between them they had £500 in readies, a huge sum at the time. In a newspaper interview many years later, Westland said that his first meeting with Ramensky produced one of the most potent memories in a long career. His 'keen sense of humour and happy-go-lucky attitude stood out'. He told an interviewer that he remembered 'a stocky man of medium build, fresh complexioned, very obviously strong and fit'. Above all, he recalled a ready smile, a nonchalant air and a perky Glasgow accent through which he joked in every situation. It was a concise and accurate description of a criminal in his heyday and enjoying it. Although they were on different sides of the law, it is clear that even on their first meeting the detective had some admiration for a worthy foe.

In the cells back at Aberdeen, Johnny told his captors how exactly he had blown the safe in the bakery HQ. The detective thought it odd that a man who had indicated that he intended to plead not guilty would be so helpful to the police. The answer was a good example of the sort of patter used by Johnny: 'Weel Mr Westland, I don't think you are the type o' man tae blab this in the witness box and if ye dae, weel after all there's just you and me here . . . And ma word's as good as yours even if I am a convicted safe blower.' Pretty much hot air, of course, and it didn't stop him from being sent down. But it shows a confidence, a lack of fear on the prisoner's part – and it underlines his lifelong ability to take on authority on its own terms and sometimes equal it.

Among the cash found on Johnny during the raid on the train at Perth was half a torn ten-shilling note, and the other half was found at the scene of the crime. When they were told of this, Johnny and de Marco both changed their pleas to guilty. Johnny got five years' penal servitude for this and de Marco got eighteen months. No doubt who was the boss on this enterprise. So it was off to the cells for Johnny, to begin planning his first great jailbreak, which would happen seven months later.

It was another four years on, in 1938, that Superintendent Westland was next to pit his wits against Gentle Johnny Ramensky. This time he was investigating a robbery at the Empress Laundry, at Seaforth Road in Aberdeen. Johnny had entered the premises through a skylight and used his gymnastic skills to swing down from the roof girders and reach the safe. It was a technique he often used down the years. He was caught in jig time by the police. On this occasion he was picked up enjoying himself with full pockets at a Glasgow club, indulging his passion for gambling big money.

This time Johnny's downfall was not a torn ten-bob note but a bookmark. The cops interrogating him found a piece of a torn envelope marking a page in a rail timetable. The laundry had kept large sums of money in just such an envelope and the bookmark had come from one of these. This and some other bits of scientific evidence made it impossible for Johnny to deny that he had been at the scene of the crime. It was back to jail to face another five years of porridge.

Back behind bars, he immediately showed a very human and responsible part of his character. He may have had years ahead of him to reflect on his crime, but his first priority seems to have been to make sure his actions in blowing the laundry safe did not result in hurt to innocent people. The day after he was jailed, 13 October 1938, he wrote to the governor of Aberdeen prison:

I was sentenced to five years PS (penal servitude) on a charge of safe blowing and attempted safe blowing on October 12. I want you to inform the proper authorities to remove a charge of gelignite which is inside the lock of the small safe. The police think the explosive was used up but it was not. I am writing because I want precautions taken so no one may be seriously injured if it did go off.

I had both safes packed with gelignite ready for firing. I blew the big safe first and on searching it I found the key for the small safe. So I put the key in the lock and opened it. I could not get the gelignite out again because once in, and round the lock, it was out of sight. I just want to draw it to your notice. The explosive might never go off, and again it may. I want to help now if I can. It was said that a charge was put in the small safe, but failed to open it. This is wrong. The charge was never exploded. I trust you will take action and prevent any accident from occurring in the future. The safes belong to the Empress laundry Aberdeen. The small safe is still in the custody of the police and can be reached in time before being sent back to the laundry office.

Yours faithfully, John Ramensky.

The letter did the trick and no one was injured. But Johnny's involvement with the man who had twice put him behind bars was far from over. Their next meetings were on matters far more important than howking money out of safes blown apart by explosives in bakeries and laundries.

# 5

# A JAILHOUSE LAWYER

In his years in Peterhead in the late 1930s, Johnny's exchanges of letters with the authorities became increasingly regular, demonstrating his knowledge of both the prison system and the law. This was the start of something of a prison career as a jailhouse lawyer which was to reach its peak in the 1950s and 1960s. In his later life in prison he showed consistent and genuine concern about the conditions of his fellow convicts. But even as early as the 1930s he was becoming an amateur legal eagle, particularly after the start of the Second World War, when Ramensky was desperate to get out of prison and do his bit for King and country.

Ramensky didn't only moan about his own conditions. One example was his concern for patients in the prison hospital. These unfortunates lost their meagre prison wages while being treated. Johnny wrote forcibly to the governor, pointing out that 'little comforts like fruit, biscuits or sweets were important especially during convalescence'. Even the prison minimum wage of three pence was important. Johnny's remarkable literacy is shown in his prison letters down the years and he was mostly using his education on behalf of others, many of whom could not read or write.

Johnny was far from the only 'prison lawyer' around – most jails had a guy who would take on the problems of others and use his writing skills to help them. It must be said that Johnny was not in the class of the most famous prison lawyer of all – Caryl Chessman, who was executed in San Quentin in 1960 after years on death row. Chessman, a mighty thorn in the flesh of the prison authorities, was nevertheless allowed the use of an empty cell (near the cell he made famous in one of his books written in prison: *Cell 2455 Death Row*). In this cell he kept his library of legal books and worked on a long correspondence with the authorities, in an ultimately vain attempt to save his own life. He also helped other prisoners write legal letters concerning ill treatment at the hands of lawyers or prison officers. The American legal system was racked with corruption and the behaviour of brutal warders kept Chessman busy in the long years up to his death.

Some of Johnny's jailhouse lawyer activities at Peterhead demonstrate how important those 'wee treats' like sweets were and how food often becomes an obsession to a prisoner. In 1936, Johnny was involved in some fraught correspondence with the prison authorities over the standard of food dished out in the jail for Coronation and Jubilee dinners.

On Christmas Day and other special occasions, the inmates of any prison in the land look forward to a rare change in diet, however slight. Anything that affects what is put on your plate is an important happening in prison. Johnny was far from satisfied with what was on the menu at these two royal celebrations. He called the offerings made to the prisoners 'starvation' rations, though the outsider, particularly in those far-off days, might wonder why such events were 'celebrated' in the prison at all.

Some of the mental strains and uncertainties in his early life are illustrated in the rather sad and petulant note to the governor, Captain J. I. Buchan, on this issue. In 1937 prisoner 3747 wrote:

Sir,
On Thursday night I was asked which I would like, an apple or an orange, on Coronation Day. I replied neither. Last year

on Jubilee Day I was robbed of half my dinner and so were all
the other convicts. I was deprived of my beef and I got a half-
pound of potatoes instead of a pound. I was given an apple to
make it up. The soup that day was rice soup which is horrible
and I never eat it. I was starving that day. I wish to protest
against the taking away of my food and ask you to consider
that if there is any cutting or slicing of diet not to take it away
from convicts who are starving enough. I wish to draw to
your notice that I lost half my dinner on Jubilee Day and I
have no desire for a repitition [sic] on Coronation Day.
Yours sincerely,
John Ramensky

This particular complaint from Johnny was given short shrift by
the medical officer who wrote in a report: 'The Coronation Day
dinner would be 10oz bread, one pint soup, 3oz of meat,
potatoes and turnip and an extra 4oz bread and a half an ounce
of marge. For the Jubilee dinner there was a deduction of 6oz
bread and 8oz potatoes but additional 3oz meat and an apple or
an orange were given.' Starvation? Not literally. Celebration
feast? No.

This episode may show a degree of concern for the physical
health of prison inmates, but when Johnny was in the early stages
of building up his appalling record of jail time, the authorities
showed little concern for his mental health. Indeed in his pre-
Army prison time it would appear that Johnny had periodic
spells of deep depression, an illness not then or now fully understood. The difference now is that it is recognised as one of the
dangers inherent in locking men and women up, and jails are
awash with trained medical personnel who can spot it and try
their best to treat it with the most modern methods. In Johnny's
day you were left in your cell with your own thoughts most of the
time without even a gruff order to 'pull yourself together' for
comfort. And if those thoughts included guilt for missing your
own wife's funeral because of your offending then so be it.

Examining Johnny's early prison records, it is hard to see exactly how, amidst the hard treatment he received at the hands of the authorities, he managed to acquire that reputation as 'Gentle Johnny'. It was a remarkable feat to keep so steady in such circumstances. But he did.

However, one event of 1937 undermines the legend that Johnny was a 100 per cent non-troublemaker. He had formed a prison friendship with a man called John McDonald who seemed to exercise a malign influence on 'Gentle Johnny'. They were accused of egging each other on to conflict with other prisoners and the warders. At the time, Johnny had his eye on a cushy job inside the prison as a baths attendant. He and McDonald were working together in the quarry pumping water one day when a fairly violent argument ensued. It was reported to the authorities by the warders supervising the prisoners' work in the quarry. This uncharacteristic outbreak of violence convinced the governor that Johnny should not get the easier job.

Perhaps this unusual aggro was understandable. Johnny was in a depression at this time, triggered by the death from septicaemia of his wife Daisy (aka Margaret McManus) back in Glasgow. Daisy was Johnny's childhood sweetheart and they had married on 7 October 1931 in St Francis' RC Church in Glasgow. They had a daughter, Marie, born in a maternity home in Townsend Street, Belfast in 1932. But for much of the marriage Johnny had been away in prison for long periods. The separation must have affected Daisy mightily. She had married a man to whom a nine-to-five job or regular work of any kind was anathema. But Johnny, too, took the separation hard.

The onset of the illness had been sudden and Daisy had died hundreds of miles away from Johnny. As he well knew, it was his own fault that he was in jail. But however realistic he was about his situation, news delivered to his cell that his young wife had died without him at her side – or even able to do anything to help in the final hours of her illness – must have been hard to take. Even for a hardened convict.

This was bad enough, but Johnny's treatment at the hands of the prison authorities did nothing to lift his depression. He made a plea to be allowed to attend her funeral in the winter of 1937. It was turned down in cold prison language as 'not the usual practice'. The ceremony was a long way from Peterhead and Johnny was said to have an unusually strong character. Strangely, a further reason was given: that he was under the influence of the previously mentioned John McDonald – though what that had to do with the fairness or unfairness of his request to attend his wife's funeral is hard to see. We can now appreciate that the prison authorities were not prepared to make a humanitarian gesture because of the perceived danger of the bereaved man doing a runner. Perhaps a cruel but necessary decision. But it fed the seeds of bitterness that ran through his days in prison in the years leading up to the Second World War.

However skilful his escape in 1934, his few hours of freedom had cost him dearly. Since his recapture he had often been at odds with the governor and his lieutenants. And the decision to ban him from the funeral ate away at him all the years that led up to his liberation and a new chapter in his life as a war hero rather than a villain. It was a deeply unhappy period in his life. His own letter-writing on the after-effects of the prison break makes it clear that from then on he nursed a major chip on his shoulder, taking every opportunity to fight on behalf of his fellow prisoners and indulging in a few feuds of his own. Later in life, when he had mellowed, and perhaps become institutionalised, he seemed much more at ease with himself.

Towards the end of his many years in prison he appeared to accept with a sort of sad, world-weary resignation, but not anger or depression, how his life had panned out. But in the 1930s there was an unsettling undercurrent of deep unhappiness in this intelligent and thoughtful man. No wonder he was constantly at odds with the prison authorities and sometimes with the inmates of the prisons he lived in.

Some insight into his thinking comes through in the letter he wrote in February 1937 to the Scottish Home Department:

Sir,

I appeal to you for fair play. On 4 Nov 1934 I escaped from Peterhead Prison and was caught and thrown into chains. Ever since I have been the victim of petty tyranny and vindictiveness on the part of the governor here. I will relate the latest and you will see for yourself. Bear with me a little and note. On November 1936 the head warder spoke to me in the quarry. He said would you like to be considered for the bathhouse job. I replied yes. He said 'very well I just thought I would ask you before anyone else asked for the job'. He added of course you will play the game. The head warder said that's all right then. The bathroom job was not vacant till Feb. 1937. In December 36 the head warder again spoke to me in the quarry. He said would I like a job as fireman in the kitchen? I replied no. He said 'you would not like it'. He then said, all right, of course I haven't forgotten the bathroom job. I said that would do me.

On February 10 the day before I was to take over my new job the head warder told me the Governor had said I was considered an unsuitable person for the job so I could not get it. I saw the governor the next day and stated my case. He admitted the truth of these facts. He also told me the reason I did not get the job. He told me that I had written a petition to you (the Governor's superiors) on Dec last and when I did so a black mark was put against me. I also wish to draw your attention to the fact that in the petition I informed you of the conditions under which a convict by the name of Kidd died. By writing to you on that matter I have again angered the governor here. Because he informed me that there was a black mark against me and I was being punished for doing so. At the same time yesterday he deprived me of all privileges on a trumped up charge of insolence. A deliberate fake. I have put up with everything these years because I have not proof. I have not written to anyone before because things do happen. But when the governor told me himself I cannot do less than see daylight. I was led on to believe I was getting a change of job, and in addition I was deprived of privileges. I have been nearly three years in the quarry. Other men do only a few months or a year and then are shifted to another job. I do not want a shift. I only want left alone. Nor do I want to be the victim to the malice or vindictiveness of the governor here. I trust you will look into this matter and help the underdog a bit. I am sir,

Yours John Ramensky.

The reference to the quarry is significant. This was hard work outdoors in all weathers, swinging hammers and breaking rock. Often this hard labour was conducted under the watchful eye of warders with rifles ready to take a pop at anyone thinking of making a break for freedom. They had done so in the past. The quarry had been in action since 1881 and conditions for those working there were, even in the 1930s, horrific. In the early days prisoners were taken by train to the quarry to break rock to be used in the building of Peterhead harbour, thereby benefiting the local fishing industry. Guards with rifles and cutlasses stood over the poor souls toiling in all weathers. In the early days the prison warders had orders to draw their cutlasses should a prisoner approach within five feet of him.

The physically punishing grind in the quarry was a job in stark contrast to others in the prison such as working in the tailor's shop, or as an orderly in the prison hospital or having that cushy number cleaning the bath area. The reference to the death of convict Kidd is also significant and illustrates the vile conditions in Peterhead at the time. It refers to this earlier letter of Saturday, 5 December 1934:

Sir,
I wish to draw to your attention to the conditions under which a convict has to fight for his life when attacked with pneumonia. Y'day Fri Dec 4 convict Kidd died with pneumonia. I do not say he died for the want of attention, but I do think he died for the lack of proper treatment and the care of those most competent to look after him. When convict Kidd died, he was in the care of a prison warder. The warder does his best. At least I hope so. But even his best, after all, does not mean very much. I bring this to your notice hoping you can do something to give a convict a chance. The same chance as every other prisoner receives in other prisons. Speaking personally, from experience, when I was unlucky enough to contract pneumonia in Barlinnie in 1931, I was immediately rushed to Lightburn Hospital, Shettleston. If I had been kept in Barlinnie I would never have pulled through. So I also believe Kidd would have pulled through. The brightness and hope which one meets in hospital helps wonderfully. The drabness of the surroundings in prison does not help a convict in his fight for life. I therefore ask you to advocate that when a convict is seriously ill to send him outside to the care of those who are highly proficient in this matter. I lay this subject before you and trust that you will give it your earnest consideration.
I am sir etc

This emotionally powerful letter may no doubt have been given earnest consideration but it did not result in much action. However, the governor and the medical officer were so concerned at what they saw as a distortion of the facts about the death of prisoner Kidd that they gave some thought to legal action against Johnny for his allegations. The whole business of prisoners taking ill and dying while in custody was becoming a huge bone of contention between Johnny and the authorities and he gnawed at the situation with regular letters. A typical example from 1937 said:

Sir,

last December I wrote you a petition concerning the death of a convict named Kidd. I received your answer 'no reason for taking any action.' Since then another convict named Gray died. I wish to draw your attention to the fact that his death was caused through neglect. Frank Gray reported sick on Sunday 21st but received no treatment. On Monday the 22nd he again complained of feeling unwell. The doctor told him there was nothing wrong with him but gave him two aspirins. On Tuesday 23rd Gray had to be admitted to hospital. He was kept there some time and finally sent outside to some infirmary. He died there. If ordinary precautions had been taken by the authorities here, that man's life would have been saved.

He was kept waiting so long in hope of treatment, and then too long in prison hospital, that the man had no chance. The only good thing I can see is that he was allowed to die outside prison. The food here is very bad and a convict has no stamina to fight an illness. Gray's sentence finished this September, a term of five years. Kidd's time 4 years was finished in four months. The longer a man is here the weaker he becomes in stamina. There is no chance for a convict if neglect is allowed to prevail. I trust you will take steps in the matter.

I am, Sir, yours sincerely

John Ramensky.

Johnny did a lot of 'I trust you will act' type of writing and no doubt these various epistles kept his active mind busy, but there is not much sign that they did anything to alter the way the authorities ran the prison. However, the bitterness in the many letters says much about Johnny's attitude at the time, an attitude conditioned by his own treatment – having been shackled and then passed over for a cushy job. That and his seemingly legitimate complaint about being kept an unusually long time working in the quarry.

# 6

# TO SERVE KING
# AND COUNTRY

In 1941–42 it was Johnny's own fate – rather than that of his companions – that exercised his mind during the long hours of confinement. As with every other prisoner, the most important date in his life was his release date. Already he was planning a new life in the Army. Like everyone else, he had read in the papers of the bitter fighting in Europe, the difficulties of every-day life in the blackout and the Blitz and the threat to Britain's very freedom.

In his cell he determined that he would help his country as best he could. This notion seemed to act as a mental balm to the sour resentfulness of a few years past. He wanted desperately to replace the helplessness of the incarcerated with action against the evil forces threatening Britain. He wanted to do his bit, as they said in those days. But he had to get out of Peterhead first, and he was faced with a release date of 12 February 1942.

It is clear that a career in the Services was on his mind. This is important because the Ramensky legend often has it that he was 'spotted' by the secret services, sprung from jail and promised a free pardon to launch his career of parachuting behind enemy lines. This is a bit of a simplification.

It is likely that he had already been spotted by our wartime secret service as a possible recruit for sabotage squads and undercover operations. His CV was perfect for that. But the legend that he was plucked from jail to join the Army is simply wrong – and tales of agents creeping around Aberdeen with their trenchcoat collars turned up and their trilbies pulled down over their eyes are somewhat wide of the mark. He finished his current sentence before he pulled on the khaki and learned to use a Commando knife to slit throats and to enjoy teaching his fellow elite soldiers the intricacies of safe breaking.

It was as early as the autumn of 1939 that Johnny wrote to his long-time literary sparring partner, the governor of Peterhead, attempting to join up. In a poignant letter he wrote:

Sir,
In this time of national need I offer my services to the country unreservedly. My parents are both Lithuanians, but I was born in Glenboig, Scotland. My father died over 25 years ago. I have a very bad record as a criminal. I assure you that most of my efforts were carried out in a spirit of high adventure. I beg you to overlook my past record and give me the chance to serve my country. I am willing to make the supreme sacrifice. I am healthy and fit in every way and I know I would make a good soldier. I have had my good times and my bad, mostly bad. Still I do not forget I owe a lot to the country I was born in. For my King and country I am prepared to do the best a man can do. Fight and die if necessary. I ask you to believe this comes from my heart. I know where my duty lies. Please give me the chance.
I am, sir, yours always,
John Ramensky.

This is not the letter of a man wanting an early release or planning an easy life. In wartime Britain, a man with his contacts in the underworld and petty crime could easily have earned big money as a black marketeer, or taken advantage of the blackout rules to continue as a cat burglar. Many inmates of Scotland's jails had only one thought – to get out and take advantage of a time when criminals could thrive more easily than in peacetime. I have met several such men who saw the war as a chance for them to thieve and plunder on a scale otherwise impossible. The prime desire of such men was to get out of jail and plunge into what they saw as a pot of dirty gold. Joining the Army and being prepared to fight and die for their country was not on their agenda.

Indeed many of the toughest from Glasgow's streets who found themselves in uniform against their will fought to get out, going AWOL or getting themselves into Army prisons and generally making such a nuisance of themselves that they were discharged. One such villain proudly showed me his papers recording an 'ignominious discharge'. He was delighted to get kicked out of the Army and back on to his home patch to take advantage of the imposed darkness on the streets and the shortages of basic foodstuffs – half a dozen fresh eggs were at a premium on the black market!

Johnny was undoubtedly of a different cut from these guys. No one could doubt the sincerity of his pleading to be allowed into uniform. And when the war was over no one could doubt that he fulfilled the promise he made about serving his country. The reality was that Gentle Johnny Ramensky did indeed know, as he wrote, where his duty lay. And he carried it out superbly in wartime if not in peace.

The letter asking to be allowed to join the Army on release was a brilliant piece of pleading but there was some legal argument about that release date still to be overcome before he was a soldier of the king. It centred round the sentence given to him at Aberdeen High Court on 12 October 1938. According to the governor he was due to be freed on 8 October 1942. This was based on the sentence minus any remission earned plus 359 days the court had passed down as a licence penalty for reconviction.

The Ramensky pen was in action as the disputed date neared. In January 1942 he thought that the argument about his release date was not in the governor's hands at all. And if that luminary was allowed to interfere with his release date 'it would be a precedent which I declare illegal'. No false modesty on the prisoner's part! He went on: 'I will not allow such an action to go unchallenged.' And he further made some sarcastic remarks to the effect that the governor knew, or should know, the correct procedure.

Ramensky had been in touch with the authorities a few weeks earlier at the end of 1941 when he gave his side of the story in some detail. He wrote:

On October 12, 1938 I was taken to Aberdeen Prison. A warder there wrote out my cell door card and on it he put five years and 359 days on a ticket of leave. What right had he to put that down when my licence was not yet revoked by the Secretary of State? Because he knew me as an ex-convict he used his authority. He was wrong in doing this.

Johnny went on to say that he had not been properly informed that he had to serve the extra days. His letters to the powers that be were becoming more and more wild and emotional, and less legalistic, and his desire to join the Army stronger and stronger. For example, he wrote to the governor:

If you support me in this argument [to agree with him the earlier release date] and say I have no licence to do you will not regret it. I will not let you down. I am fit in every way to be a member of the armed forces. Will you give me this chance? I know I have a very bad record, but are you game to take a chance? You cannot lose by it. You will also have the satisfaction of knowing that the country has gained another soldier who will fight to the last.

In all this he won one fight and lost another. He lost out on the earlier release date but he was winning his battle to serve king and country. On the day of his release, a typically brisk and cold north-eastern day, he called on the CID chief John Westland in his office straight from the jail. This was not as surprising as it seems, for the pair, despite being on different sides of the law, had begun to become friends and shared a mutual respect. The journalist John MacLellan told of the meeting in a *Daily Mail* series on Johnny's career. The visit to the police station was Johnny's first move on coming out of prison and he was soon eating bacon and eggs at the police chief's desk.

Johnny was always aware of what was going on and very astute. On this occasion he noticed many more casual visitors to the chief's office than would normally be expected. He quickly twigged that the visitors were young detectives who didn't know Johnny and had been told that if they popped in they could have a good look at the infamous safecracker.

Putting aside the ham and eggs, he turned to Mr Westland and said: 'I am surprised at you.' The detective asked what was wrong and Johnny said, 'Why don't you call them all up and introduce me to them properly!' The detective recalled the incident with some embarrassment but went on to tell of his role in getting Johnny into the Army. At this meeting Mr Westland asked Johnny to confirm his wish to join the Army and told him that he would do everything he could to help. Johnny explained that he feared his criminal record might work against him and put an end to his desire to join up in the fight against Hitler. To help out, the Aberdeen police chief wrote a long report to MI5 explaining how the released prisoner could be of use, underlining his expertise in breaking open safes.

For a long while the police and intelligence services had been aware that Johnny could be of immense help in the war effort. Now it was finally going to happen. Westland asked Johnny one more question – would he give his word of honour that as long as he was in the Army he would go straight? Johnny gladly did so.

This episode is another example of Johnny's liking for authority figures such as Mr Westland, his Army commanders, prison governors and senior detectives both in the north-east and in Glasgow. He seemed naturally able to engage intellectually with such men and strike up friendships with them, sometimes friendships that lasted for years.

While still in prison, but with Army service on his mind, Johnny Ramensky decided it was time to sort out his troublesome name once and for all. It had been at the root of too many problems in jail and he did not want those problems to follow him into the Army, if and when they allowed him to join up.

So, while still behind bars, he began a campaign to become simply John Ramsay. The whole Ramanauckas/Ramensky/Ramenski/Ramsay business was a mess. In the past he had at times informally adopted the name John Ramsay. Clearly any such campaign for an official change by deed poll would require the backing of the prison authorities but at least he had his stated desire to fight for king and country to help his cause. And on this occasion Ramensky found the authorities willing to help.

Johnny's letters to the authorities on the subject underline that chip he had on his shoulder about his name. For example, in August 1942, writing as prisoner 3870, he told the Scottish Home Department:

I would like to have the name John Ramensky altered to John Ramsay on my identity cards and ration cards. That is the name I should be under here [in Peterhead]. When I was arrested over four years ago I gave the name John Ramsay to the police. They said, 'oh, no you are John Ramensky to us' and I was indicted under that name. If the police had taken the name given to them first I would be John Ramsay today. My reason for a change is that it would enable me to make a fresh start in a few weeks time. I intend to join the Army. I have waited a long time for it and John Ramensky would not give me a fair chance in the Army. It is uncommon and I feel certain bound to attract attention of someone who otherwise would not know me as a man with a past.

Other reasons are; I was married under the name John Ramensky Ramsay. My wife is dead now. Her name was Daisy McManus. I have a little girl registered as Marie Ramsay. It would be thought strange if I was in the Army under the name John Ramensky. I was married on October 7, 1931, at St Francis cathedral [sic] Glasgow. I had to go to Glenboig, Lanarkshire for my baptismal papers and take them to the priest. I was married under the name John Ramsay and would like to carry on under it if possible. I would be very much obliged if it could be arranged. I would not be ungrateful.

I am, Sir, yours sincerely

John Ramensky

This letter was forwarded to the appropriate authorities by Governor Buchan who added that Johnny frequently asserted his desire to join the Army as soon as he was liberated. He added that he appeared most anxious to keep clear of prison in the future and that: 'His conduct and industry have been excellent since he was sentenced on 12.10.38. He is due for liberation on 8.10.42. I recommend that if at all possible Ramensky's request should receive favourable consideration.' It seems the good Captain Buchan, for all the hassle Johnny had given him down the years, was not a man to bear a grudge.

A few weeks before Ramensky's release, Governor Buchan wrote to the Prisons Department saying that Ramensky's National Registration Identity Card had been changed to Ramsay and that the Ministry of Labour in Acton, London, had been told, but that the name change would not apply to existing prison records. Peterhead officials also helped him in writing to the National Registration Office in North Silver Street in Aberdeen about the complete change of name and the correspondence was sent to New Register House in Edinburgh. The transition took some doing.

In reality, however, and despite his desire to be known as

Ramsay, he was simply so well known that many continued to refer to him as Johnny Ramensky. However, he did manage to get married as Mr Ramsay and his daughter was also named Ramsay, so at least he had managed to change his name for future generations if not for himself.

So it came about that a man who was to become a brave patriot and one of the most famous Commandos of the Second World War would begin Service life under a new name – John Ramsay. He used it in its full official glory almost for the first time on the day of his release. After his chat with John Westland, he travelled south to Rutherglen, just outside Glasgow. On arrival, he visited the local police station to tell them about the name change and about his desire to join the Army and do some serious fighting and safecracking for his country. Johnny was such an infamous character that Chief Constable Keith of Lanarkshire made a report that 'John Ramsay' had turned up at that Rutherglen police station on 8 October 1942 flourishing the paperwork that confirmed his change of identity. A new and adventurous chapter was beginning for the boy from Glenboig.

# 7

# THE GREEN BERET

From short trousers to his final days in prison, an unquenchable desire for adventure flowed through Johnny Ramensky's blood. The Army, for him, was never going to be life in a quiet base peeling spuds and whitewashing walls. In his fight to join up he had described his early safecracking and cat burglary as being 'carried out in the spirit of high adventure'. However unpalatable this was for the victims of his life of crime, it was true and it was obvious that his natural military home was with the newly formed and highly daring Commandos.

Fate may have played a hand in making him a round peg in a round hole in the Army, but there was considerable human intervention as well. Shadowy figures in MI5, John Westland, and the top men in the Scottish Prison Service combined to ensure his destiny was to be fulfilled. Initially Johnny joined the Royal Fusiliers, a London regiment (not the Royal Highland Fusiliers) in what seemed a purely administrative move. On officially joining the Fusiliers in Glasgow on 19 January 1943 he was given his Army number, 6482307, and posted to Achnacarry House, Spean Bridge, Inverness-shire, the Commando training HQ.

Aside from the allocation of a number, he must have felt there were other similarities with his prison days. His kit was issued with the bureaucratic efficiency of the prison service attending to a new convict, and in the Army, as in prison, no detail was too small to go unrecorded. The Fusiliers issued Johnny with the following: blouse, trousers, denim overall trousers, shirt, vest (woollen), drawers (woollen), drawers (short cellular), jersey, jerkin (leather), socks, cap/helmet, boots, anklets.

His papers admitting him to the Army say his 'apparent age' was thirty-seven years and eight months, his height five feet six inches and weight 152 pounds. His chest measurement was thirty-eight inches when fully expanded and the range of expansion was three inches. Complexion was fair (no mention of a prison pallor – no doubt work in the Peterhead quarry saw to that!), eyes blue and hair fair. His religious denomination was RC and he was in A1 health.

Like many prisoners, Johnny took a pride in his fitness and worked out whenever possible. Prisoners these days, if they are inclined, can pop down to the prison library and spend long hours losing themselves reading literature, 'improving' or otherwise. But before the Second World War there was little educational input. Hence the desire of those serving the long sentences so common in those days to maximise any opportunity for exercise. Despite his constant complaints about the prison diet, Johnny had acquired a relative fitness in prison that would help him in the Army.

From the Fusiliers he had been selected for training with the Commandos, the elite military force set up by Winston Churchill in 1940. Its orders were clear – to harry the Axis forces and regain the initiative in the war by raiding the enemy-held coastline of Europe. Its motto, 'United We Conquer', was particularly apt for Johnny. At last he was at one with a group of men, volunteers in a dangerous war, men who would stop at nothing in a no-holds-barred battle against a dangerous enemy. Here the old taunts of 'Lithuanian' and 'foreigner' were forgotten. He stood side by side, as John Ramsay, with British fighting men united.

Many of his colleagues had rather different backgrounds from his own – many had been volunteers from the regiments and corps of the British Army. But some others in the Commandos had also seen 'action' in pre-war civvy street. Within weeks of being formed, groups of Commandos were blowing up trains, planting bombs and creating mayhem as best they could behind the lines in Europe. And later in the war they fought in the Far and Middle East. All this was something of a dream come true for Johnny – in the Army he got the excitement and respect he craved. Plus the acceptance of his fellows, whether they came from factory or public school or the prisons of England.

The structure of the Army suited his temperament perfectly. Already partially institutionalised by his years of prison time, he fitted effortlessly into the regime. He was able to impart to others his illegal skills with gelignite, safes and locks of all types, while at the same time enjoying the intellectual challenge of acquiring new military knowledge. And all the time he was meeting, and being part of, a wider society than he had ever met behind bars in Scotland's toughest jails. Or even at the bar, shoulder to shoulder with the toughest of the tough in Glasgow's many rough pubs. He even got paid. And the food was better than he was used to.

Coincidentally, in 1942, the year Johnny changed his name and ended years of confinement in north-east Scotland, the Commando Basic Training Centre was established in the Scottish Highlands at Achnacarry and some other sites in the north-west Highlands. It was here that the Commando soldiers, who came not only from the British Army but also from the Royal Marines and the Allied Armies, honed the dark arts of Commando fighting. These were very hard men, specially selected to carry out some of the most dangerous tasks of war. There was a rigorous selection process and only those who survived and thrived in the training in the snow-covered peaks and glens of Lochaber qualified for the accolade given to the Commando – the famous Green Beret. The beret was the hallmark of the highest standards of military training, self-discipline, physical endurance, initiative and bravery. Those who wore it wore it with pride in themselves and their companions and enjoyed remarkable comradeship. The uniqueness of this band of brothers is illustrated by the fact that they were awarded eight VCs. One thousand seven hundred Green Berets lost their lives in the Second World War and many others were seriously wounded. Churchill was grateful and said of the Commandos: 'We may feel sure that nothing of which we have any knowledge or record has ever been done by mortal men which surpasses their feats of arms. Truly we may say of them, when shall their glory fade?'

After training in Lochaber, an awesomely beautiful place in summer or winter, John Ramsay earned his own hard-fought place in this remarkable group. He had persistently made it known to all and sundry that he wanted to put his expertise in explosives to good use in the interests of his country.

The officer who interviewed him and enlisted him into the elite squad was a remarkable man known as 'Lucky Laycock'. Robert Laycock was in his early thirties when he was called upon to form and head 8 Commando in 1940, one of the first of the special units that would be regarded as a model for armies of all countries from then on. He was a tough guy and looked the part with a boxer's nose and eyes set wide apart. He was married with five children and had attended Eton and Sandhurst, a rather different background from most of his recruits. Indeed, it is said that he was the model for Evelyn Waugh's character Lt Colonel Tommy Blackhouse in the novel *Officers and Gentlemen*.

Laycock had served with the Royal Horse Guards and worked behind a desk in the War Office before the call came to form the Commandos. He had the initiative and daring to be the man to mould and lead the Green Berets. It was a special job for a special soldier and Laycock's wife Angie seems to have summed him up correctly when she reportedly said he had a 'rare combination of upper-class nonchalant panache and professional efficiency'.

It is not too hard to imagine such a character taking a shine to a likeable rogue with a Lithuanian background who had spent years in Scotland's toughest jails and who liked nothing better than a nerve-tingling romp across a darkened rooftop in search of a safe to blow apart. In London, soon after his release from Peterhead, Johnny was taken by the intelligence services to see Laycock, then a brigadier. This was part of the process to get Johnny into the Commandos – first he had to join the Army as a Fusilier and then he had to be transferred to the new elite group if they decided they wanted him. In the interview the pair had a long chat about Johnny's civvy street experiences.

Laycock was decisive. 'I am going to give you the chance of being a Commando. I am sure you will do well.' Johnny muttered his grateful thanks and said, 'I'll do my best.' Later he recalled the legendary Commando's response. Like a flash Lucky Laycock snapped back: 'Your best won't be good enough. You will have to do better than that.' But Johnny was in and on the way to a career in uniform.

After this, Ramensky went back to Glasgow to the Moffat Street recruiting centre, where he pitched up unannounced and said he had been instructed to go to the Commando training centre at Achnacarry. This took the staff by surprise as he had been in the Army for such a short time. It was highly unusual but north he went.

The secretive training given to the new soldier John Ramsay and his colleagues was remarkable. In the early 1940s vast swathes of north-west Scotland had been designated a 'protected area' by order of the Home Secretary. Permits were required to pass through checkpoints at road crossings along the line of a natural water barrier formed by Lochs Linnhe, Lochy, Oich and Ness, and the Caledonian Canal. All this was happening without the knowledge of the folk who lived in the far-off Lowlands. The War Office had a more or less free hand to select areas and big houses and estates to use for this vital training. The local aristocrats threw their hand in with enthusiasm and it is said that

Simon Fraser, the 17th Lord Lovat, personally selected Inverailort and a number of other smaller houses as the site for the training school. The area was ideal – rugged country and a broken coastline suitable for small boat work and assault techniques. The sparseness of the local population was also useful as live ammunition was used in training to add realism.

The Highland railway ran nearby and provided access for troops and supplies. It also came in handy for dummy demolitions as the Commandos learned the art of sabotage. Today, thousands of tourists a year swish effortlessly up the hills above Invergarry heading west, pausing for an occasional flask of coffee or a photo opportunity at the many laybys on this fine road, and get out to stand high above one of the most beautiful pieces of country in Europe. You wonder if they have any idea what it was like here in the early 1940s. It's unlikely, given how little trace has been left behind.

The trainee Commandos, including Johnny, were a remarkable crew. Johnny was there to pass on his expertise in controlled explosions but he also had to learn the essential skills of armed and unarmed combat – including the use of the famous Commando dagger to slit throats and silently dispose of luckless Nazi sentries. The art of neck-breaking was also taught. The lecturers in this University of Dirty War included Freddy Chapman Spencer and Martin Lindsay, polar explorers and experts in Artic survival. Also involved were former Shanghai police officers William Fairbairn and Eric Sykes, who were experts in close-quarters pistol-shooting and knife-fighting. A lot of deadly expertise was being shared. It all must have come as a bit of a shock to the man already known as Gentle Johnny – for in this new world it was kill or be killed.

The Commando dagger, which also became their motif, was in fact designed by Fairbairn and Sykes. It was produced by Wilkinson Sword who, aside from their fame as razor-blade manufacturers, had made the blades for swords used by the British Army for generations. In all probability they made the blades for the cutlasses used in the Peterhead quarry in the old days. The dagger was double-edged, with a seven-and-a-half-inch steel blade and a brass hilt. It could be used as a survival weapon as well as being deadly in knife fights. It was particularly useful for killing with a thrust to the carotid artery in the neck. The Commando, with his face blackened, would creep silently up behind an unwary foe and with one silent thrust of the 'F-S Fighting Knife' there was one fewer soldier to do the bidding of Adolf Hitler.

At Commando school in the mountains of Lochaber, the men who were at the forefront of the battle against the Nazis were taught to have no scruples. There were no prissy ideas about fighting fair on the agenda. And it was a strength-sapping slog. They were certainly not playing cricket, old boy, in these wild mountains, as the hardest men in the British Army prepared to be parachuted behind enemy lines.

The toughening-up regime typically started each day with reveille at 6.30. On most days, even in the coldest of winter, the soldiers wakened to the skirl of a piper marching through their Nissen hut playing loudly enough to waken the dead and leaving the doors at each end open to the howling, biting Highland wind. Right away the men were off on a training run (about a mile) at 7.00, followed by PT, breakfast at 8.00, parade at 9.00 and inspection. Usually the morning was topped off with a route march of eight to ten miles (with arms, in battle dress) at a fast pace. This included cross-country work, map reading, compass work, moving through cover and the like. There was a bite to eat at 1.00 and then from around 2.30 the group had a session of ninety minutes of swimming, running and exercising. The numbing snowmelt water that filled the lochs was, it appears, not specially heated for them. Tea was at 4.30 and it was usually was followed by a forty-five minute lecture at 5.00. The evening after 6.00 was free for personal time and company duties. If you had the energy.

At all times the troops were expected to rally at the blast of a whistle or horn and come running out of their billets. Each man carried a flask of whisky and 'morphia' tablets as part of his kit. He also carried a short length of rope with a bight at one end and a toggle at the other. These ropes could be joined together for climbing cliffs or for making rope bridges, or as safety lines to help cross fast-flowing rivers.

Commando training was not always a serious, no-laughs business. And it did not stop Johnny enjoying himself and certainly retaining that most important characteristic that impressed all who met him, his sense of humour. An ambulance driver from the Clackmannanshire area recounts an interesting tale. His team was called to uplift a sickly old fellow to take him to hospital. One of the routine checks made by the ambulance crews is to ascertain that the patient has a referral letter from his GP. This patient said he had and added that his doctor was a German and remarked jocularly that maybe he was the only German he had met that he hadn't killed. A good starting point for a lively chat with an old soldier. It turned out that he had been a Commando during the Second World War and had seen a fair share of action. The Germans the old patient met in those days were not the friendly sorts. The former Green Beret told the ambulance guy that he had trained in the Highlands and that he had bunked for a spell with a soldier who he thought was Ramensky – though he remembered him as John Roman 'or some name like that'. The old fellow might not have remembered the right name, but he was impressed by what a 'likeable' guy Johnny was. He used the word several times.

After training, their paths in the Army had separated and surprisingly the ex-Commando mentioned that he often wondered what had happened to his roommate after those hard days exercising in the snowy Highlands. Obviously the old fellow was not a great newspaper reader. When Johnny was in his heyday, there was hardly a literate Scot who had not heard of him! The ambulance man enjoyed a good crack with the ex-Commando on that journey to hospital and, in particular, they both pondered the irony that a man trained in the black arts of combat, daggers in the dark, explosives and the sudden demise of German soldiers, should end up being well cared for by a compatriot of his former foes, working as a medical practitioner in Scotland.

Johnny himself had happy memories of his training. He recalled his first shock when, after drawing his uniform and equipment, he found that he was to bunk with twelve ex-policemen. They were training to be instructors and he found them a friendly bunch, despite his background. But the many years he had spent in jail up to that point in his life meant that Commando Ramsay needed a little specialised training of his own. He was put under the watchful eye of a Sergeant Major Robertson. These days it would be called mentoring, but back then Robertson's task was simply to turn Johnny into a soldier. Johnny said that hour after hour, day after day the sergeant major drummed into him the basics of foot and arms drill, the details of who to salute and how to do it, and who to address as 'Sir' and how to recognise the badges of rank. Many a time he saw fellow soldiers watching curiously as he and the sergeant major conducted what was a one-man parade. The ex-safecracker loved it all. The feeling was great, he said.

The training was a hard test. After all he was almost twice the age of some of his training colleagues and when they had been building Army careers he had been languishing in prison cells. But on 8 March 1943 he made it. He got his Green Beret.

After Scotland he was moved to a Commando brigade HQ in Dorset, where he learned even more about explosives. He also taught his fellow Commandos and wrote a treatise on the various techniques of safe blowing. This work led to a tour of Army establishments lecturing on safe blowing and giving general demonstrations of work with explosives for sabotage. One of the bases he visited was the Special Operations Executive (SOE) camp at Beaulieu in Hampshire. There he was watched with admiration as he cracked a selection of safes that had been specially assembled to help him show the SOE trainees how to do it. His students picked up some of his skills but in the front line there were certain safes that could only be opened by the master himself.

By a strange coincidence, one of the places Johnny dispensed his knowledge to fellow combat soldiers was at Noranside, near Forfar in Angus, then an Army camp, later a sanatorium and a borstal and now an open prison. During one of his post-war conversations behind bars with 'Sonny' Leitch, Johnny told how he used to enjoy eating a raw sweet chestnut, plucked from an ancient tree in the grounds. Sonny, later an inmate in Noranside, found the tree still in the grounds and enjoyed a wee treat chewing a nut from it and thinking of his old pal.

But for Johnny Ramensky real war was approaching and soon he was on a Navy vessel heading for Italy. There, at one stage, he was billeted with Commando colleagues in the Villa Nobile, in a village near Florence. During his time there he met and befriended a Welshman called Dennis Whitcombe, now a sprightly ninety year old who looks more like he's in his sixties. Whitcombe recently told his local newspaper, the *South Wales Argus*, that Johnny was one of the bravest men he had ever met. He also mentioned Johnny's numerous disappearances from the main group for a day or two at a time. The surmise was that it was a secret mission or two that required his special skills with 'gelly' and his ability to open lockfast premises.

It is interesting that Dennis, something of a war hero himself, remembers the striking difference between Johnny's appearance and his lifestyle choice as a career criminal. To the Welshman, Johnny was an ordinary-looking bloke who did not resemble his 'master criminal' legend in any way whatever. It is an observation echoed by most people who met Johnny in civvy street.

Dennis Whitcombe also thinks that the group involving Johnny could well have provided inspiration for Ian Fleming, the author of the James Bond novels. Fleming was a habitué of the smoke-filled clubs of London's Pall Mall, where some of the

Commandos' most outrageous clandestine operations were discussed and planned over brandy and cigars. And he met many of the characters in the Commandos who were closely involved in a dangerous secret war. Johnny was in good company, with Robin Hood, Papillon and a touch of James Bond for comparison!

If Johnny's story was an inspiration to Ian Fleming, the author was not alone. The Hollywood actor Ray Milland directed a film starring himself as a safe breaker in 1958, the very year Johnny broke out of Peterhead three times. The plot has a strong link to the Ramensky story. In *The Safecracker*, Milland plays a criminal who is rescued from prison by an Army officer and offered a deal – if he will go on a dangerous mission behind enemy lines he will be given his freedom. The mission is to break into a Nazi safe and steal a list of German spies operating in Britain. He agrees and is trained as a Commando and parachuted into occupied Belgium on what one film critic called 'the caper of his life'. *The Safecracker* was said at the time to be 'supposedly based on a true story' and it certainly has a familiar ring. A year or so before it was made, it is said that Hollywood types were spotted nosing about in the north-east of Scotland. The idea of criminals being sprung from prison and their skills used by the Services seems to have a strong fascination for filmmakers.

Back in the real world, in Italy, Johnny trained as a parachutist, learning how to leap safely from many types of aircraft, at many different altitudes and in all sorts of weather. This was all to ready him for the challenges of working behind enemy lines with the partisans. It was a challenge he was to conquer in spectacular fashion.

When the physical torture and excitements of training in the Scottish Highlands were at last just a memory it was time for 'live' action. One of the most important escapades Johnny took part in involved him and his fellow Commandos suffering a frustrating few weeks. Even he, a man of iron nerve, said that the suspense got to him and nerves he wasn't supposed to have twitched. His group was trying to get behind enemy lines near La Spezia, a major Italian port, situated between Genoa and Pisa.

Their mission was to help Allied bombers silence huge German guns protruding from mountainside tunnels. They were part of an impressive fortress built by the Germans to command the country lying beneath the base, and control the road to and from Rome and the approaches from the sea. These mighty weapons were hindering the Allied advance from the south. High above the gun emplacements, the hills had been dug out for trenches to be filled with machine guns and all sorts of traps to safeguard the big guns.

The original idea was to parachute behind the lines and send information back about the German positions. This expedition suffered from the problems that always seemed to hinder parachute operations in Italy, Germany and occupied France. The difficulty was transporting the spies or agents of sabotage to the right place at the right time. In those days aviation was not the precise business it is now. Aircraft often wandered around the drop zone in darkness and low cloud unable to find the exact point for the drop, sometimes under fire from the ground. Even when they could find the drop zone there had to be enough light for the paratroopers so that they could land safely. They also had to be wary of an ever-vigilant enemy. Anything suspicious on the ground which suggested an enemy ambush would mean calling off operations for the night. It was a risky business and the responsibility to deliver the Commandos to their destination in a fit state to carry out their mission was, of course, paramount.

So it was in the adventure at La Spezia. Time and time again the Commando paratroopers hauled themselves into the plane, blacked up, nerves jangling and ready for action, only to find themselves back at home base after the pilots had been defeated by the weather or military intervention. These delays forced a change of plan. The new idea was that Johnny and nine collea-gues, commanded by a Lt Robinson, were to make their way through the enemy lines on foot from positions much further away from La Spezia than had originally been intended. Another group, commanded by Lt Russell, was to be dropped by parachute nearer the guns and join up with the squad already on the ground if at all possible. The advance party, a desperate bunch of men, all had pistols and silencers and a box of ammunition. Maps of the area were provided, drawn on silk – a life-saving handkerchief. If by any chance the fighters were caught they would have to rely on an escape kit which included a small saw and a compass. In a pragmatic nod to the old notion that money talks – especially in wartime – they all had a huge wad of Italian lire notes.

The first part of the journey was taken in cars along roads to the north from a special headquarters in an area under Allied control. The Commandos were dropped there at what was essentially the front line of a battle between the advancing Allied forces and the Germans and Italians. American tanks were sending shells screaming towards the enemy in the hills. The Germans pounded back at the advancing troops below. Faced with this battleground, the Commandos soon realised what they were up against and that their route to the big guns was directly across the hills held by the Germans.

The British boys had been set down in the midst of an area held by a division of black Americans, some of whom were wild and desperate characters who carried revolvers looped round their waists like Western gunfighters. This would come naturally to these guys who were part of the 92nd infantry division – the famous Buffalo Soldiers – the only group of black men to fight at the front in the Second World War. The Commandos took off on their mission in the dusk, watched by the black American soldiers.

Johnny reported that: 'All of us were loaded like camels. In a rucksack on my back I was humping at least 70lb of food, explosives, sleeping gear and other gadgets.' The Brits also carried Tommy guns and generators, particularly heavy, for the radio sets. The destination for this group was a cave where they had information that Italian resistance fighters were hiding and waiting for them. As they struggled towards some form of safety in the dusk it was still light enough to see the big guns in the hills and the menacing machine-gun nests around them.

When they finally joined up with the partisans it was so dark that nothing could be seen or heard but the hellish sound and sights of savage warfare – flashes of the German guns in front of them and the Allied guns behind them. This was the front line and it was a long way from Lochaber. Or Peterhead and Barlinnie. But this was what the fierce training had all been about. There was much sweating and swearing in the dark as the party climbed towards the mountaintops. Confronted by a sheer cliff face, Johnny edged to the left to go round it and others in the party took to the right. Suddenly there was an explosion followed by cries of agony as some of the partisans aiding the group were hit. The path to the right had been mined and by sheer chance Johnny had taken the path to the left. Luck had saved him. A handful of partisans had been badly injured and some of the group's equipment damaged, including radio batteries. It was no place to wait around. Some partisans were left to tend for the wounded as best they could, and the others pressed on hard over the peaks towards dawn and a dangerous descent on the other side of the mountain.

Coming down was as demanding as the ascent. Here on the eastern slopes, away from the Mediterranean sun, the snow and ice still lay thick and one mistake with your footing could take you off the narrow paths and over a ledge to sheer drops of hundreds of feet. It was similar to the terrain the Commandos had trained on in Inverness-shire and the group were thankful for the skills they had developed in winter conditions in the mountains of Scotland. Eventually they reached the comparative safety of the valley below. They were finally behind the lines and overjoyed at making it alive.

They ate a hearty meal in a hiding place shown to them by the partisans and slept the day through. That night the Brits needed to contact base to report, in code over crackling radios, the damage to their equipment and ask for replacements. Johnny himself cranked the generator and eventually they picked up their 'signature tune' on a special wavelength. They asked for new supplies and then waited.

After a couple of days nothing had happened and there were no new supplies forthcoming. Two soldiers were then delegated to cross back over the enemy lines with a message. They made the dangerous journey successfully and the group was told by radio to light seven fires in the shape of a cross when a plane flew over that night. It was all to be another huge disappointment. A plane arrived and droned around for a bit, but despite the fires being lit it disappeared with no sign of a parachute drop. The Commandos and their Italian allies were desperately disappointed. Food was now low, with only a few sweets and energy tablets left. And the battery would not respond however hard it was cranked.

There was no alternative but to move on in the direction of La Spezia and the target. Goats and chicken were killed for food with the silenced pistols and the saboteurs lived off the country, again reaping the benefits of their training. But the journey was marked by two horrors. The first was the shock of seeing what was by now a ghost town called Montone. The partisans had ambushed a German there and killed him. This sparked retaliation by Nazi tanks and there was huge devastation in the picturesque little town. Montone was also, later, the site of a bloody battle between the advancing Allied troops on the road to Rome and the defending garrison.

The sight of the place that day had a huge effect on Johnny. The devastation he saw upset him terribly. He wrote that as they passed through this village there was only one human being in sight – a German sentry on a bridge. The Commandos resisted the temptation to kill this lone soldier, something they could have done with ease. But as they pressed on they must have collectively wondered about the innermost thoughts of this fellow soldier as he kept a vigil over a dreadful scene. It was an image of all-out war that was to stay with Johnny for years.

All that was more than fifty years ago and Montone is now a tranquil tourist attraction high in the hills. It is unseen from the main Italian north-south road which runs nearby, thronged with tourist buses and holidaymakers moving between the beach resorts and the cultural and tourist attractions of ancient towns and cities. But Montone was far from alone in suffering reprisal attacks by what Johnny called 'the Hun' in his post-war interviews with newsmen back in Scotland.

The next horror of war encountered by the Commandos as they headed north came at Vinca. Here was proof positive of the ferocity of the German reaction against the Italian partisans. At Nuremberg the war crime trials would later be shown letters from Hitler and Kesselring to the troops, urging the shooting and hanging of locals who had attacked the invading Germans or hindered them in any way. The savagery of this policy and its utter disregard for the old rules of war in the treatment of civilians were barbaric. One German death was to be revenged by the killing of scores of innocent civilians.

This ruthless attitude was personally encouraged by Hitler, who additionally wrote in a memo to his commanders in October 1942, after being told how much trouble the Commandos were causing in Italy, that saboteurs and agents were to be slaughtered to the last man. Wearing the Green Beret was a dangerous occupation. Oddly, in this memo Hitler made the distinction between what he regarded as 'real' soldiers and Commandos. It was the old German military thinking kicking in – on the battlefield you took prisoners and treated them with the respect a warrior deserved. Commandos were a different breed to be killed immediately.

I therefore order: from now on, all enemies on so-called Commando missions in Europe or Africa, challenged by

German troops, even if they are to all appearances soldiers in uniform or demolition troops, whether armed or unarmed, in battle or in flight, ARE TO BE SLAUGHTERED TO THE LAST MAN. It does not make any difference whether they are dropped by parachute. Even if these individuals, when found, should apparently be prepared to give themselves up, no pardon is to be granted them on principle. In each individual case, full information is to be sent to the OKW [Oberkommando der Wehrmacht ('Supreme Command of the Armed Forces')] for publication in the Report of the Military Forces.

This chilling edict was signed by the Führer. Vinca was a classic example of this ruthlessness in action. Partisans had killed two German soldiers and the Nazis moved in and selected every girl aged between fourteen and twenty and shot them. Some were dragged from their beds or their parents' arms and in all 120 were slaughtered. Johnny remarked that it was no wonder the partisans they worked with were ruthless and gave no thought to the taking of a German life. He sympathised with the Italian partisans, who had suffered both from the Germans and on occasion from the Allies.

As they neared La Spezia, four Allied planes were heard droning above an enemy-occupied town called Sarzana which they could see clearly lying below their mountain hideout. As the Allied bombers swooped low Johnny and his colleagues could see the bombs falling onto the town below. Huge columns of smoke rose in the sky and after one load of bombs had fallen the planes swooped round again to throw more explosives at the town. Soon there was little left to destroy. But the planes were by now diving down and raking what was left with machine guns and cannons. Witnessing this horrific scene was one of the partisans working with the Commandos. His wife and family were down there under the hellish pall of smoke.

It was too much for even a tough guy like that to watch – he screamed that the planes must be shot down, collapsing and weeping in anguish. Johnny later told the interviewers back in Scotland after the war that they never discovered what had happened to their friend's family but that he stayed with them, a staunch fighter against the Nazis. Such experiences must have been traumatic for a man like Johnny who eschewed even the violence of Glasgow's streets. This was the stuff of nightmares. The bombers were doing their job and many a pilot must also have had to wrestle with the thought that the bombs that killed Germans and their collaborators also took the lives of resistance fighters and locals on the ground. And maybe even some of our own secret agents. Collateral damage, so common in war reports these days, is nothing new.

By now the Commandos were getting within range of the target. The good news was that they had re-established radio contact with their base. The next step was a vital airdrop of supplies. Mussolini had planned to build an airbase in the area and this uncompleted site was to be the target of the first drop. The area chosen was on a plateau and signal fires were set. There was deep snow around, the hillsides were icy and there was little shelter for the frozen Commandos who were by now seriously short of food and supplies. After three nights there with nothing happening they were joined by the second Commando group, who had made their way through enemy lines. Then, at last, the sound of a plane was heard and an officer shot a Very pistol into the fires that had been built. Each had a little explosive in it, planted by Johnny, and soon there was a circle of fire to guide the aircraft. The plan had finally worked and down from the sky came food and drink, weapons and ammo, cigarettes and money.

But, hungry as the men were, food had to wait till the next day as the real business of the whole operation got into full swing. During a snatched bite or two at the new rations the Allied air forces were radioed with the information they needed to help them blow apart the big guns of La Spezia. The Commandos had a ringside seat at what must have been one of the most memorable and dramatic sights of the war.

The huge guns that were holding the Allies back rolled in and out on rails from tunnels in the mountainside. It took many raids and much accurate bombing, helped by the information coming from the Commandos, to silence them. It was a hard task for the bombers but with the aid of the Commandos and partisans it was accomplished. The road north was opening up and the race to Rome and Berlin on. Considering what had happened at La Spezia it seems singularly apt that, at the end of the war, the port became a major point of departure for the survivors from the concentration camps. It is said that from the middle of 1945 to early 1948 more than 23,000 Jewish prisoners left Italy secretly for the Middle East.

Following the action at La Spezia, Commando John Ramsay and his comrades were straight back into explosive action. Although the Allied aircraft had pasted Sarzana almost into the ground in that horrific aerial attacked, witnessed by the Commandos and the partisans earlier, amazingly one building had survived. This was the HQ of several hundred fascists who were collaborating with the Germans. This did not please the local partisans and one Italian guerrilla called Walter called on the Commandos in their secret hiding place with a simple request – blow this HQ and its hated inhabitants sky-high. Naturally, the first man to call on was Johnny and he reckoned that it would be a relatively easy hit, provided he had all the details he needed. As in his old trade as safe blower, he was meticulous in finding out every last detail of a target and planning accordingly.

The situation was this: the building was on the corner of a busy square into which six streets ran. On the ground floor was a massive timber door typical of such places and there was always a guard on duty. A significant number of fascists slept two floors up in what they thought was the safety of a large dormitory area but Johnny identified this as their weak spot as it had windows on more than one side of the room. He planned to somehow get a large bomb off the ground and up to a height of twenty or thirty feet. The idea was to push the explosives up to the windows with a large pole and hold them there. It was a dangerous plan but the partisans agreed to it.

Ramensky then went over the detail of how this was to be done. He would stuff 60lb of plastic explosive into empty sandbags which had each been fitted with guncotton primers and an instantaneous fuse. The bags would be tied together with string and more fuses. All this was carefully calculated to give the HQ a massive hit but not damage nearby buildings or harm innocent neighbours. The explosive devices were attached to fuse runs of thirty feet or so and switches arranged so that there were two means of setting the bomb off. To Johnny it all seemed simple enough – when the partisans got the bombs in position they would throw the switches and have a couple of minutes to get to safety.

But Johnny had one major worry. He was concerned that the partisans might panic and not get everything right. He shared this fear with his commanding officer and got the reply he wanted – he was to accompany the guerrillas on their mission and set the explosion off himself.

A twenty-strong party set off from the Commandos' hiding place at dusk, carrying the bomb slung on poles. Two men took turns to carry it on their shoulders. On the outskirts of Sarzana, another twenty partisans joined the heavily-armed group as they crept towards the target. The barking of dogs was a problem and Johnny himself had to despatch them with his silenced pistol. It was not a job he enjoyed, but this was a life and death mission. When Johnny's group and the local reinforcements met, the locals had provided a tree to carry the bomb rather than the poles. And when they came to a house roughly the same height as their target, they tried to haul the tree and the bomb upright to test whether or not it would really work. It was just as well that they did. The combined weight of the bomb and the tree that was to hold it in place was too great for them to manage and the tree had to be sawn down to a size that was strong enough to carry the weight of the bomb but light enough to lift. However, despite the difficulties, the bomb was eventually raised into place.

When they arrived at the square the partisans posted men on each of the corners with machine guns to control entry. The rest of the group crept around the shadowy side streets where the HQ was. By this point Johnny's original fears were coming true: the tension was getting to the partisans who were becoming more and more excitable. They began to argue among themselves about who should have the honour of setting the bomb off. But the argument was cut short by the ominous and unmistakeable rumble of a German truck heading for the square. At this point the partisans took to their heels and ran back towards Johnny. Among them was the man who had to pull the switches but he assured Johnny everything was fine and the fuse had been lit. It was time to cut and run.

When they were no more than a few hundred yards from the HQ a huge explosion lit up the town. A few yards more and there was another explosion. This was not in the script. It later transpired that the two bags of explosives had split apart when they were being hoisted up to the window, as the partisans panicked at the sound of the approaching lorry. It was a disappointment for Johnny. If the two bags had gone off together the HQ would have been destroyed. In the end the building was only damaged and only one Blackshirt died though several others were injured. But it was enough to scare the fascists into a more secure new HQ in a local castle with a moat. And in this case the Nazis took no reprisals against the civilians. As Johnny had predicted, the behaviour of the partisans had compromised the mission. But it was just a small disappointment in a long war.

Around this time, left to his own devices, Johnny was coming up with some cracking ideas on the sabotage front. The Germans relied a lot on trains to move supplies and troops around Italy.

Blowing up a train or a bridge was an attractive proposition, but the Germans were getting wise to the business of protecting their trains. They implemented a policy of putting a couple of empty wagons at the front of the train so that any explosives on the track were detonated by the empty wagons. This left wreckage that was simple to push aside and it was relatively easy to repair the track and let the supply trains get through. Johnny came up with the idea of a trigger fuse that was activated when the wagons passed over it, but the actual explosives were then further down the line ready to explode directly under the locomotive.

The Commandos set up a trial and it was a great success. They watched with great delight as a huge locomotive was blown high into the air and completely blocked the track. This was a major blow to the Germans' transport system as the occupying forces were short of the heavy lifting equipment that was needed to clear then repair the track. Indeed this was, from the Allied point of view, more productive than blowing up bridges or viaducts. With those it was not too difficult for the enemy to rig temporary repairs and open the line in a short time. Hundreds of tons of locomotive straddling the rails was far harder to cope with.

Not all of Commando John Ramsay's time was spent hiding in caves with partisans, creeping out at night to blow up targets or radioing valuable information to the Allied air forces. In 1944 he was able to take some part in the reoccupation of Rome and had the pleasure of walking the streets and squares of the Eternal City, by then filled with flags welcoming the Allied forces. He especially seemed to enjoy the streets filled with young Italian beauties dressed in colourful floral prints, with a smile or more for the Allied soldiers.

But war was war and German stragglers still hid around the alleyways of Rome ready to pick off careless soldiers. Capturing these snipers and others was part of the mopping-up process. One of the Germans picked up by Johnny and his pals turned out to be from the Goering School of Espionage and Sabotage and he let slip that all the saboteurs had been supplied from the German Embassy in Rome. This called for immediate action and the Commandos raced to the embassy. Johnny was among the first through the gate and they headed straight for an iron door in a high wall in the garden, acting on information garnered from their captive. 'Go ahead, Ramsay,' barked the major in charge as Johnny strained at the leash to get at the lock that secured the door. The door was secured by a large padlock, no deterrent to the man who liked to say he had never been defeated by a safe, however complex. It took seconds to open the door, which led to a flight of stairs down into a dark cellar.

Great care was taken, since this was a perfect place for booby traps, but Johnny made it to the bottom and was able to shout back up the stairs: 'Here it is, sir. It's all here.' What a hoard – stacked on the floor around the large cellar were heaps of metal drums filled with TNT, plastic explosive and gelignite. The shelves around the walls were stacked deep with all sorts of bomb switches, fuses, booby-trap devices and incendiary gadgets. It was, remarked Johnny, a saboteur's paradise.

Back up the stairs in daylight, the party found a lone Italian standing at the edge of a newly dug hole no doubt intended to hide explosives. In nearly every building in the embassy grounds, the soldiers found grenades or explosives of every kind imaginable. There were also a number of rooms with safes containing they knew not what. Johnny was the man to open them. But while he was busy on one a huge explosion rocked the whole place. The major and Johnny looked at each other for a moment and then raced towards the underground explosives depot.

Their first concern was that some of their lads had been caught by the blast but none seemed to be around. Later it emerged that by luck they had all been on the other side of the thick garden wall at the time. But a quick glance down the steps into the cellar showed a fearsome scene. The drums of explosive were scattered around and several fires were burning. Every few minutes there was a small explosion as a grenade or small bomb went off. At any time the whole lot could have gone up, tearing the embassy apart and taking a good chunk of Rome with it. The soldiers set to work immediately to control the fires, moving heavy cases, some containing 500 detonators, and using extinguishers from their lorries and any other fire-fighting equipment they could lay their hands on. With the immediate danger over, the Commandos racked their brains to work out what had started the explosions, but they never came up with a satisfactory explanation. If it was a booby trap, Johnny concluded, it had been set by an amateur – otherwise he and a good few others would be dead.

It seems that when wandering the corridors of the embassy the soldiers stopped to pocket the odd souvenir from the lavish lifestyle of Goering and his cohorts, who dined in style on the best of food, and swilled fine wines in huge rooms filled with furniture worth millions. Some amusing little pieces of evidence on this turned up in the research for this book.

A Mrs Cook, now living in Dundee, told me that her father had a shop in Regent Street, Rutherglen, near where Johnny's sisters lived in the 1940s and 1950s. When not serving one of his sentences, Johnny would pop in for a chat with Jimmy Love in his dairy-cum-grocery. They had both lived in the Gorbals in the old days. Anyway, if there was a few quid owed to the shop by his sisters, Johnny always paid up when he was in for a chat. And, no doubt a tad guilty that he spent so much time away from the family behind bars, he would urge Jimmy to keep an eye on his relatives and assure him he would never be out of pocket.

Mrs Cook remembers an act of kindness with a historic touch. Shortly before he was locked up as a result of one of his final safe breaking adventures, Johnny gave Jimmy Love a serviette as a wee gift. This was no ordinary serviette – it was beautiful silk decorated with a black swastika and came, claimed Johnny, from one of Goering's 'palaces'. Maybe the last time it was used was to dab the stains of a fine claret from the lips of someone in the German High Command! It is still something of a Cook family heirloom in its new resting place, Scotland.

However it has to be said that much more spectacular were the memorabilia shown to me by Dorothy McNab in Rutherglen, where Johnny and his family spent many years. Indeed despite moving house many times, they were never far from the Main Street of this famous old burgh on the south-east of Glasgow. The douce Rutherglen of the 'Wee Red Lums', which feature in the title of a famous play performed by the old Rutherglen Rep, held a lifelong attraction for Johnny. But that did not stop him 'tanning' a local bank or business if he thought he could get away with it. That curious complete lack of conscience, so obvious in career criminals, allowed him without a second thought to rob his fellow residents of this friendly wee town which once ruled its own affairs, complete with town hall and local theatre, before it was swallowed up by Glasgow. Dorothy is Johnny's niece, a lively lady of a certain age with a great sense of humour and still enjoying life to the full with her pals, despite the odd health problem. She has lots of stories of family life with the Ramensky/Ramsays.

One day as we sat in her neat and well-kept home, nibbling chocolate biscuits and sipping coffee together, she opened a box of souvenirs (normally securely stored in the bank) of Johnny's Army days to show me. It was a strange experience to hold his hard-earned Green Beret – size seven and a quarter – and speculate on the action that this battered headgear had seen. Well worn, it still bore the marks where, over the years, it had been pinched by thumb and forefinger as it was placed on the head, at a cocky angle. There was also his trusty compass issued back in the training days in Lochaber, but much used to navigate around the mountains of Italy in the company of partisans in the behind-the-lines actions. Like the Green Beret, it had a well-used appearance. Dorothy also had his maps of the La Spezia area, which had been printed on fine silk and could fold away into a tiny little square of material. A handkerchief with attitude!

In her little 'treasure box' was a fine collection of cap and khaki blouse badges, often featuring the famous Commando dagger symbol, and well-shined brass buttons. His dog tag too, from the time he joined the Royal Fusiliers, was there with his name Ramsay and the number 6482307. The box also contained a couple of items that had no doubt graced the desk of some top Nazi in Rome before finding their way into the kitbag of Commando John Ramsay – a brass paperweight of the famous pre-war German liner the *Bremen* (the pride of the Norddeutscher Lloyd Line and the German merchant marine, and one-time Blue Riband holder) and a medallion with the visage of the fascist Mussolini looking stern.

But the most impressive and dramatic souvenirs are two large silk banners. The theory is that they had come from the walls of Goering's headquarters, Carinhall, on the Schorfheide estate, or maybe even the German Embassy in Rome.

Johnny's raid on Carinhall was one of the most audacious episodes in the Second World War. He was reputed to have been parachuted into the target area on a secret mission to find out what the strong rooms of this grand place contained. Intelligence chiefs were delighted when the wiry little safecracker from Scotland handed them secret Nazi plans on a plate. The effect of the success of this mission, or its difficulty, cannot be underestimated.

It is doubtful if all the facts of the raid will ever be fully known. That the Commandos breached Carinhall at all is remarkable. It was one of Goering's many HQs, named after his first wife, and was a suitable home and sometime wartime HQ for a man who, as well as being the second-in-command in the Third Reich, gloried in the title of 'State Forestry and Hunting Master of Germany'. He also had a state residence on Leipziger Platz in Berlin, various other hunting lodges and a couple of castles he had inherited. But Carinhall, where his first wife, a Swedish divorcee Carin von Fock-Goering was entombed, was a favourite. It had a room devoted to hunting trophies, naturally, and a cinema and a bowling alley and a *Bierstube*, again naturally! It also stored Goering's massive miniature railway, a toy for him to play with in moments away from the strain of trying to dominate the world.

Deep underground, Carinhall also had a sinister bunker where, no doubt, military plans and looted art works were stored. The walls were eight feet thick and the place was almost impregnable. It even boasted a squad of firemen thirteen strong and was guarded day and night by security men and crack Nazis troops. That the Allies managed to gain entry at all was a tremendous and audacious feat of war.

It was a strange sight as Dorothy unfolded the lurid red banners in her home – it all seemed curiously out of place in peacetime Scotland, almost shocking; powerfully and strangely evocative of the days when the leaders of the Third Reich strutted Europe. There was no sound of jackboots on the march in that Rutherglen sitting room, nor any brass bands, nor crowds outside thunderously chanting, *'Heil Hitler'*, but you could not help but hear them in your head.

Around six feet long, the banners look to be designed to hang vertically on a wall, perhaps behind a desk. One is pink, carrying in embroidered letters the slogan: *'Der Reichsmarschall des Grossdeutschen Reiches'* ('Marshall of the Great German Empire'). On the reverse side is a delicately embroidered eagle, its talons sitting atop a black and white swastika. The other banner is deep red silk with a legend, this time printed rather than embroidered. On the front it reads: *'Oberbefehlshaber der Luftwaffe'* ('Commander-in-Chief of the Air Force'). On the reverse again there is an eagle above the swastika. Ramensky's war trophies form a fascinating collection.

But during Johnny's sojourn in Rome the serious work was opening embassy safes rather than seeking out ammo storage depots. Over the years, this has become an integral part of the Ramensky legend, though it seems to have been somewhat exaggerated. There is no doubt whatsoever that he carried out valuable work in the German Embassy in Rome, though some claims cannot be substantiated. For example, it is said that he blew open a large number of safes belonging to many of the major figures in the German High Command, even those of Hitler himself.

When Johnny was with 30 Commando, he seems to have transferred from one Commando group to another from time to time and he was part of a group that operated ahead of frontline troops gathering intelligence to aid the Allied forces after the invasion of mainland Europe in 1944. These sorties were known as 'assault intelligence missions'. One version of the legend has it that as the Eighth Army moved across North Africa it became imperative to learn what Field Marshall Erwin Rommel was planning next. And Johnny is said to have recovered documents that gave the war effort a massive boost when he cracked the Desert Fox's safe at Sidi Rafa in the Libyan desert.

What is beyond doubt is that his service records do list him as having spent time in Africa. His Military History Sheet reads as follows:

Home. 19.1.43 to 24.3.44. 1yr 66 days.
N. Africa. 25.3.44 to 12.8.45. 1yr 141 days.
Home. 13.8.45 to 23.2.46. 195 days.
British Army of the Rhine. 24.2.46. to 25.6.46. 122 days.
Home. 26.6.46 to 10.9.46. 77 days.

It would appear from this list that the North Africa acted mostly as a base from which to travel to Italy. The same document, signed by a W. Edwards of the Army Records Office in Ashford, Middlesex, records that Ramensky was released into the Army Reserve on 11 September 1946. It is fascinating that when he moved from the regulars to the Territorials, one of the forms he had to fill in asks if he is British. His reply is: 'Yes. (Scottish.)' He was ahead of his time in making a distinction so many Scots use today when faced with forms on planes or at passport controls.

Under the heading 'Medals and Decorations, Clasps and Annuities' in the History Sheet is an ink stamp entry saying 'Awarded War Medal 1939–45'. There is no mention of the award of the Military Medal, a claim which was frequently dropped into newspapers articles about his war service. His next of kin is given as his mother Marie (using the Anglicisation rather than the Lithuanian Mare) Ramensky, then living in Polmadie Street in Glasgow's Southside. The History Sheet also records a couple of minor disciplinary matters. In August 1945 he was confined to barracks for eight days for being absent without leave for thirty-six minutes after midnight. Apart from the AWOL, a second charge was 'being out after curfew'. You wonder what mischief he was up that night. Thirty-six minutes does not seem time for even such an adventurer as Commando Ramsay to do much damage!

Perhaps because of the secrecy of war, and especially the covert operations Johnny Ramensky was involved in, many questions about his true wartime role remain unanswered. His was a secret world where his skills could finally be used for the good of the country. But what is the truth about his wartime safe blowing exploits?

One of the world's leading experts on safes and safe blowing, a Glasgow man who writes under the name of Peterman, has some pertinent observations on Ramensky's Rome adventure. In particular he has reservations about tales that Johnny blew twelve (some reports say fourteen) safes in a day in Rome. Peterman writes:

> None of these claims have ever been verified but are at the highest end of improbability purely on points of technicality. Embassy safes, and those of military importance, would have been of the highest security grade in their country of origin

and fitted with at least one keyless combination as general practice. In the case of embassies the use of the combination lock would have been to enable a secure changeover of the senior diplomat in charge, the key lock being used for daytime use by staff without the time-consuming procedure of having to dial up the combination lock, the primary use of which is for overnight protection. I had experience of this in 1948 when called to what had been the German Consulate's offices in Glasgow. The Consul's safe was a Bode-Panzer fitted with two combination dials. The locking system was known as Lafette whereby one of the lock dials was a dummy, controlled by the other true lock, concealing a pull-out stem behind the dial with a breech device at the inner end into which a small key bit was inserted and returned into the lock mechanism to operate as would a normal key by turning the dial. This system therefore had the same effect as having a keyhole shutter operated by a combination lock which was the British method of preventing an explosive charge from being placed through the keyway into the lock.

Confusion over the word 'safe' could be behind some of the inconsistencies in the legend. Peterman is of the opinion that on occasion the correct description should be strong room rather than safe. He points out that the great weight of conventional safes makes it unlikely that large numbers like twelve would be found in upper rooms in an embassy or indeed any commercial building. It is indeed quite common for such places to have book rooms with 'security cupboards' rather than what the layman would call a safe. In his opinion Johnny could indeed have broken into twelve or so of such protected structures in jig time.

It is doubtful that the full details of what went on in the German embassies and Army HQs at the end of the war will ever be known, but Peterman's theories seem plausible and they are given validity by the fact that when Johnny spoke to reporters about this after the war he mostly talked about 'working' on the safes rather than 'blowing' them. This could confirm the Peterman belief that the twelve-safe tale often quoted in the legend is a trifle extravagant – though there is no doubt that Commando Ramsay could lay claim, at his peak, to being the top safecracker, or peterman, in the world.

Another clue to what really happened comes in Peter Haining's well-researched book called *The Mystery of Rommel's Gold*. Haining says that after getting into the 'safes' the Commandos left as quietly as they came, which suggests that explosives had not been used. Even Johnny could not create a silent explosion, though he was a master of using as little explosive as necessary and muffling the sound. Perhaps this is what happened in the embassy in Rome and Johnny was edging iron baffles aside with tiny blasts rather than blowing locks apart. But none of this speculation and mystery can in any way tarnish his reputation as the best when it come to using gelignite or tumbling locks open.

There is an intriguing little postscript to this tale of the raid on Rommel's HQ. It could have been much more successful than it was and could have dramatically changed the course of the war and, indeed, history. The Commandos were after documents held in this particular place, not fully aware that Rommel spent much of his time at this location, though they knew he did wander around various hot spots of the desert war. Hours before the Commandos arrived on their secret mission to blow open the safe in search of battle plans, Rommel had been staying at this HQ and could have been captured or killed during the raid. But, on a whim, he had decided that day to move up to the front line and share the dangers of battle with his troops in bloody action. It was the sort of move that made him the brilliant commander he was and helps explain why the men under his command revered this old-style German military man. A brave action by a fighting general, it probably also saved his life.

# 8

# TOO LATE TO GO STRAIGHT

For Johnny Ramensky, crime was always a game, sometimes played with very high stakes but always played by the rules. As his life progressed it became increasingly difficult to change his ways or his chosen career path, but his generally good conduct saw to it that the majority of his dealings with authority were on good terms. He just couldn't ever manage to give up the excitement and the thrill of his work.

It is said that racing drivers get hooked on the adrenalin rush that comes when the green start light comes on. They find it almost impossible to retire. So too did the master safecracker and jailbreaker, who positively thrived on the excitement of rooftop chases and outwitting the warders trying to keep him behind bars, a man who would plot an escape for weeks or just as likely seize any passing opportunity to slip his bonds. So perhaps his attitude to the police and prison staff is understandable in the sense that they and Johnny, and his pals, were all players in a big game.

Certainly in Johnny's case slipping into friendship with people on the other side of the law happened many times. The most classic example is John Westland, who, as recounted earlier, played a major role in getting him into the Army on his release from Peterhead. Other instances include a friendship formed with the Peterhead governor, J. I. Buchan.

Harvey Grainger, a retired journalist living in Aberdeen, tells some interesting tales of Johnny's friendships. Harvey's father, also a journalist with the *Press and Journal* in the 1930s and 1940s, often reported on Johnny's headline-grabbing escapes. Grainger Senior enjoyed telling his son that when Johnny used to return from an escape, or one of his heroic excursions behind the enemy lines, it was his habit to bring home a wee present or two for one of his adversaries in the police service, such as Detective Inspector Slatter, late of Aberdeen CID. On one particular occasion Harvey's father remembered a valuable watch being handed over. It had not, one suspects, been bought over a jeweller's counter!

Harvey himself, in turn, ran into Johnny when he was sent one day by his picture desk to photograph the escaper's capture in Aberdeen after one of his most famous breaks from Peterhead. To Harvey and his dad, like hundreds of folk in the northeast, Johnny was something of a folk hero.

It could be argued that Johnny showed classic symptoms of bonding with his captors. Jim Ironside, a former prison officer in Peterhead, provides a further example. By the time Jim took up work in the north-east jail Johnny was back in Glasgow doing time in Barlinnie, and certainly not escaping with the frequency that had made him a Peterhead legend. But he was still well remembered and well talked about in the long, cold nights in the echoing halls up north in what is perhaps Scotland's grimmest jail. Jim recalls that at Christmas a card would arrive addressed to 'Staff, HM Prison Peterhead'. It had been posted from Barlinnie down in Glasgow and carried the simple signature *Johnny R.*

Another example of Johnny's no-hard-feelings policy towards the cops comes in a quote from the late Bob Colquhoun, a well-remembered detective superintendent in Glasgow, who shared Johnny's love of good clothes and was a bit of a dapper dandy in his heyday. Bob said: 'Like most policemen who have come in contact with Ramensky I found him an engaging character, the kind of man who, applying his brain to another, more acceptable, type of occupation would probably have made good.'

Once, when Johnny was in prison, word came to him that the copper who had so often pursued him was seriously ill in hospital. Johnny got a message to Bob Colquhoun to convey his good wishes for a speedy recovery and made the observation that maybe the detective had taken too much out of himself chasing him around Glasgow after a safe or two had been cracked. An oddly kind thought exchanged between criminal and cop.

A sometime contemporary of Bob Colquhoun was the legendary crimefighter Les Brown who rose to the top of the Glasgow detective tree after starting his career pounding the beat in the Gorbals of Johnny Ramensky. He remembers: 'During the late 1950s whilst on the beat we, the cops, manned a crossing opposite Bridge Street subway – not far from the Ramensky home in Eglinton Street. During my stints I was approached by a middle-aged woman who introduced herself as "Mrs Ramsay". [This was Johnny's second wife Lily.] It was winter and very cold and she handed me a hip flask, which contained rum, which I drank. The flask was handed in to the staff at the subway office to be picked up later by Mrs R. Most of the cops on the same duty got the same "gift".

'During a conversation with her I asked if there was a "Mr Ramsay". She said there was and I asked what he did and she replied, "He is doing time in Peterhead Prison." So I asked what for. "Safe blowing," she replied.

'Knowing most of the safe blowers operating at that time I told her that I had never heard of a safe blower called Ramsay and she said, "Oh, that's not his real name – you would know him as Johnny Ramensky." I'd most certainly heard of him!

'I remember, too, another similar episode. During one of his escapes from prison we were detailed to mount a watch on his house in Eglinton Street opposite the Coliseum Cinema, top flat right. What the bosses didn't know was that such a watch during the night shift was made bearable by Mrs Ramsay supplying the cops with hot drinks. It was an easy job because if

Johnny was on the run he was much too smart to call in on Lily.'

Les Brown added: 'Months later I was on foot patrol in the Gorbals when I was approached by Ramensky, who shook my hand and thanked me for our dealings with his wife. I asked him, tongue in cheek, if he was out officially, and he assured me he was! You could never be sure . . .'

Johnny's almost total lack of animosity towards the cops is further illustrated in a tale told by Dick Lynch, a retired barber who worked at Hagerty's shop, now long gone, in Eglinton Street. Johnny often popped in for a trim when not in jail. After the almost obligatory reference to how smart the old lag kept himself when on the outside, Dick remembers a friendly fellow who always left a good tip and was well aware of his infamy in the district, but who was never other than discreet about his activities when talking to the man with the scissors. They say women confess all to their hairdressers – not Gentle Johnny Ramensky.

Almost sixty years later, Dick Lynch remembers the old days in Eglinton Street well – the old Coliseum cinema and the famous NB Loco amateur boxing club. On many a morning, he saw the great safecracker standing at the corner of Bedford Street and Eglinton Street, passing the time of day in a friendly manner with the local constable or police sergeant if he happened to pass that way. When at home in the Gorbals, Johnny was always ready to chat with the boys in blue, except maybe in the immediate aftermath of a night on the tiles, as you might say.

Johnny's little penchant for dropping gifts to his friends on the other side of the law caused something of stushie during the war. Even amid the torrid dangers of life as a Commando behind enemy lines in Italy, Scotland's north-east was not far from his mind. He took the trouble to write to John Westland, the detective who had been so important in getting him into the Army, at every opportunity. In the letters he made it clear how happy he was in the Services and how he was enjoying what he regarded as a great adventure. He also found time to send picture postcards home to his sisters in Rutherglen. Being a Commando satisfied his thirst for thrills and, though he was putting his life on the line on a daily basis, the risk of death or capture, and perhaps torture, at the hands of the Nazis only seemed to add to the buzz he got from being in uniform.

One pencilled letter to Mr Westland in the autumn of 1944 was accompanied by the gift of a cigarette box. It read:

Dear John,
I send you this cigarette box in remembrance of our friendship. I am doing well here in Italy and hope you are the same. With all best wishes

In fact there were two cigarette boxes – or 'stands' as Johnny called them – and the other was for the governor of Peterhead prison, Captain J. I. Buchan, a man with whom Johnny had a somewhat turbulent relationship, though in the end it seems neither man bore a grudge. In a PS to that little pencilled note to Mr Westland, Johnny explained he couldn't send the box direct to the governor 'as it would cause talk'. He asked the detective to pass it on, which he did.

But the gift caused more than talk. There was considerable correspondence among the authorities over its fate. The governor, of course, played by the rules and declared the gift. Captain Buchan was then told that when he acknowledged the gift he should explain to Ramsay that he was 'precluded from accepting gifts and in these circumstances he has passed on the box and its contents to . . . who will benefit from Ramsay's generosity, without of course, knowing more than it had been gifted by a Commando serving on the Italian front'.

All done by the book, but shortly after this note to the governor came a rare change of mind. The prison authorities had relented and Governor Buchan was told that in the special circumstance he could accept the gift. One suspects that maybe the news of the brave work Ramensky was undertaking on the front line had filtered upwards in the corridors of power. Whatever, the gift was accepted, though Captain Buchan was told to tell the Commando hero that such gifts were not normally allowed and he was not to do it again.

After this little episode the letters home stopped for a while. Johnny was busy cracking safes, looking for enemy secrets and helping the partisans with plans to blow up a Nazi supply train or two. But he did write to Mr Westland in May 1945 explaining his recent silence on the letter-writing front. He had been away for twelve weeks on a mission, he explained. He had only just returned and there was a stack of mail waiting to be dealt with. He said it had been an exciting time – that word again – but, of course, the Official Secrets Act did not permit him to go into any detail. That had to wait until the war was finally over.

However, he did impart a piece of important information. He told his friend that 'Jerry has had it and by the time you get this it may be all over'. He was spot on: within weeks the war in Europe had ended. The future beckoned and Johnny reflected that his mother was happy about his recent way of life in the service of his country and that made him happy, too.

So that was it – an end to a few years of fighting shoulder to shoulder with Commando colleagues and with the partisans, and breaking into safes more challenging than those normally found in bakers' shops and small-town bank branches. The enemy, too, would change in future. No longer would he be taking on Nazi stormtroopers and collaborators. The enemy again would be the boys in blue. But that was not to happen before John Westland, a man with a real interest in Johnny's welfare and rehabilitation, made a last attempt to lure him onto the straight and narrow.

Before his demob, Johnny spent some time stationed in Lubeck, where his eastern European background and linguistic skills could be used to help the thousands of displaced persons in the defeated Germany. Several camps in the British Zone, created immediately after the war, contained some of the 70,000

Lithuanians who had reached the West. Lubeck had its share. And there were also many Polish refugees, with one camp alone holding more than 1,200 people who had fled to the West.

John Westland, coincidentally, was also in that war-torn area, on special duty involving policing, and he was in the position to offer Johnny a job back in civvy street. It was, he said, a real chance to break with the past. He was saddened when Johnny shook his head and turned the opportunity down. It seemed inexplicable that the war hero, a man who had thoroughly enjoyed an adventurous life away from prison bars would say no to the chance of a new start. But Johnny had his reasons. It was not until eight years later that John Westland got the full story. Eight puzzling years. But the sad truth was that the offer of a job had come too late – Gentle Johnny Ramensky had already filed John Ramsay, Commando, into a special drawer in his mind and returned to his destiny – a life of crime and further long spells behind bars in Scotland's prisons.

9

## ON THE RUN AGAIN

When Johnny changed his name to Ramsay and joined the Commandos he had promised his sponsors one thing: when in the Army he would be the straightest of straight arrows. By and large he was true to his word – though to keep it might not have been too hard for him. In civvy street, boredom – and the need for gambling money – had been a driving force to send him safecracking and breaking into homes and premises. During the war he had found himself getting his daily ration of excitement handed to him on a plate. In the Commandos his practical knowledge of explosives qualified him as a teacher of the black arts. By all accounts he was a skilful tutor, able to share his knowledge with ease. It won him the respect of his colleagues. He was *the* expert and his commanders acknowledged his unique skills. 'Leave it to Ramsay' was on many occasions the solution to a difficult problem faced by his fellow soldiers. His commanders had faith in him.

On demobilisation, you might assume that the bravery and the acclaim given to him by the men he fought with would have been an incentive to stay clean and try to build a new life in the harsh post-war world. It may have been an incentive but it did not work. In signing him off, that famous military man Lucky Laycock had written to him in the following terms:

Dear Ramsay,
Now that you are leaving the Army Commandos I would like

to add to the many messages of farewell you will be receiving from your contemporaries and friends my own personal thanks to you for the part which you have played in this war. May your gallant service to your King and Country be rewarded in the future by peace, prosperity and happiness.

Yours sincerely

R Laycock

Chief of Combined Operations.

There is more significance to this letter than meets the eye. Laycock was a major figure in Commando history and, as we have seen, the man who helped recruit Johnny. He was clearly appreciative of Johnny's war service. There is not a smidgen of doubt that he admired Johnny's work and his war record. Yet astonishingly in 1959, many years after the Ramsay Green Beret was consigned to a drawer in his home, questions were raised in Edinburgh about John Ramsay's deeds in the Commandos.

This was in part caused by the fact that in his final months in the Army he had been an officer's batman, something that did not quite square with the legend. But there was nothing sinister about this. With the shooting, sabotaging and safe breaking part of the war over, he stayed in the Army for a further twelve months. And his Army records show that not too long before he was demobbed he was transferred from the special engineering unit (a nice Civil Service description for men who generally created mayhem and fought outside the rules) to an Infantry Battalion. So there was nothing irregular in giving him the job of batman – a trusted aide to a senior officer. Sniffy remarks about this part of his Army service were off the mark. But the legal establishment in the late 1950s seemed to have tired of his war heroics being endlessly trotted out in court in pleas of mitigation. Even the then Scottish Secretary seemed to suspect the lily was being gilded a little by Johnny himself and by the legions of newspaper feature-writers who had chronicled his exploits.

The truth, of course, was in the official records which were released forty years later. These showed that although there are still some mysteries and untold tales –because of the inevitable secrecy surrounding some of his missions – basically the legend of Gentle Johnny Ramensky is fact.

As a result of the questions raised by John Maclay, the Scottish Secretary of the day, about Johnny's war service, one part of his story was publicly proved wrong. As previously noted, he did not join up till he had finished serving his sentence. The secret service did not arrange for him to be plucked from Peterhead and given a promise of a pardon. That apart, there was nothing to deny the basic facts and it was not Johnny's fault that newsmen eager to spice up a story had got that particular aspect of it wrong.

Another inaccuracy is likewise not his fault. The story that he was awarded the Military Medal is clearly wrong, although some sources say he turned it down. But there is little significance in that fact either. To the thousands of Commandos, the Green Beret was regarded as a medal and they wore it with pride. If every Commando who deserved it had been given a medal the manufacturers would have been on overtime for years.

The arguments in Scotland about Johnny's war service drew the War Department into the saga. What they had to say on the matter is conclusive. In a letter from the then Secretary of War, signed by R. M. Hastie-Smith, it was stated: '6482307 Fusilier John Ramsay served in the Army from January 1943 to September 1946. He was enlisted in the Royal Fusiliers and was employed by the Commandos on special duties including parachutist duties until July 1945. I am afraid I can not give you any details about his career in the Commandos but clearly there is an element of truth in the story of his military career.' There is also on the record a letter dated 12 July 1945, signed by a Captain Bamber of 30 Commando, which states: 'John Ramsay. The above named soldier is being posted (to the Fusiliers) from this unit on disbandment. He has a satisfactory record of service with the unit and has taken part in assault intelligence missions behind the enemy lines. He is a qualified parachutist.' That exposes the nasty sniping from some in the Edinburgh establishment, whose idea of adventure was sipping decent claret with luncheon in their club and an afternoon polishing the bottoms of their pinstripe trousers, for what it was – inaccurate, spiteful rubbish.

These sceptics were, as they say in the Army, not fit to lace the boots of Commando John Ramsay. And their cynicism was a disgrace. It was an astonishing episode and almost unbelievable that the Edinburgh establishment should doubt the veracity of the story of a remarkable life, and doubt it to the extent of writing to the War Office to question it.

The reference in the Laycock letter to the friends he made is important. Johnny had a real talent for engaging with all sorts of people, inside and outside jail. There are countless stories of what good company he was and how easily he could slip into communities or groups. Peace, prosperity and happiness are not, however, words that are appropriate in the ongoing story of the boy from Glenboig, the likeable rascal, who had so famously and bravely served his country.

For Johnny Ramensky, the days after the Second World War did not go the way that Lucky Laycock had hoped. There weren't even a few years spent with his feet in front of the fire, and a relaxing read at the racing press he loved. No, Johnny was back in his old ways even before the train from the south transported him back to the Gorbals!

He explained this many years later to John Westland – indeed this was the real reason he refused the job that day in Lubeck. Johnny had concealed a secret from both the Mayor of Lubeck – who had accompanied Westland to the meeting in the refugee camp where Johnny worked – and from the detective himself. The old lag had already pulled a job or two. Indeed, his first thought was that the Aberdeen detective and the Mayor were in the camp to question him about certain break-ins in Wrexham,

Norwich and Colchester back in the UK. The offer of a job was not what he was expecting. Johnny had pledged to go straight when in the Army, but squared this with his recent criminal activity by saying that when his Commando unit was disbanded in 1945 he felt freed from his promise. When these break-ins took place he was on leave, just waiting for his official discharge. By then he was not a Commando, merely batman to an officer.

In fact, it is remarkable that all Johnny's exposure to violence and the dark arts of killing in secret did not seem to affect him after the war. Despite the detailed and rigorous training in the dirtiest of dirty work he was still, on demob, Gentle Johnny. There is no doubt he used the expertise picked up in the Highlands to good effect, but back home he reverted to his old style. If his collar was felt he went quietly and took his punishment as a man. This is a real tribute to his strength of character. Many an ex-soldier took to violent crime on demob, sometimes even using weapons stolen from the service. Some former squaddies would even use their time as fighting men in uniform as an excuse in court for their violent ways in civvy street. Not John Ramsay. His modus operandi remained unchanged by his experiences in the war. Safebreaker, yes, natural born killer, no.

Having refused an offer to go straight, Johnny Ramensky soon landed back in jail, this time in York in 1947. Back in Glasgow, out of uniform, he had started a new career as a bookmaker. He was too exuberant a gambler himself to succeed at that business – though he had several attempts at making a go of it. One prison governor had commented on his gambling in a memo. The gist was that Johnny should not be compared in any way with the 'shilling each way' punter; that he was a man who got a buzz from gambling hundreds at a time. Risk-taking with cash, as well as his life, was in Johnny's blood.

In the post-war years, when not in jail, he was a well known figure in such places as Glasgow's infamous Gordon Club, a haunt of big money men like bank robber Dandy McKay (also a prison escaper), Mendel Morris and Arthur Thompson Snr. You need a lot of cash to sustain a lifestyle like that. No doubt some criminal contact had convinced him in 1947 that a wee spot of the old excitement in York could provide the opportunity of an easy hit on a safe or two full of readies.

According to press reports of the time he was caught 'red-handed in a store at midnight' in the act of blowing a safe. The adrenalin must have been flowing that night. His long-time friend Tom Clark was with him. Johnny pleaded guilty to 'breaking into premises and placing explosives in a building with intent to destroy'. His war record was mentioned in court and described as impressive, though it was noted cynically and accurately by the prosecution that, 'it is clear he has not taken long to revert to a life of crime'. However, his Army record may have played a part in the sentencing. Johnny got five years while Tom Clark, who was described as a bookie's clerk, got seven. Ex-Commando Ramsay was not happy at this: he loudly informed the court that Mr Justice Singleton, who had handed down the sentences, was 'a heartless old scoundrel'.

# 10

# A GIRL CALLED LILY

In the years after the war, back in the Gorbals and Rutherglen, Johnny had won himself a girlfriend, an attractive widow called Lily Mulholland. In their letters there is real tenderness and they had many happy times together, though it was only little more than a year after they met that Johnny was in England and in jail. Lily styled herself as Johnny's fiancée in 1947 and they eventually married in 1955, the delay mostly because of Johnny serving time.

Lily was always in his corner fighting for him and, after he was jailed in England for the York job, she worked hard with a local MP, Dick Buchanan, to get him transferred to a Scottish jail. Johnny and Lily were very concerned about his mother's state of health. Johnny in particular was fretting about lack of contact with her and his inability to see her doctors and hear about her treatment first hand.

Letters on the subject of his possible transfer flowed between Lily, the MP and the prison authorities on both sides of the border. One note in the archives tartly remarks that because of his swift return to crime after the Army: 'Ramensky does not deserve very much consideration'. After some correspondence and various pleadings for a move on humanitarian grounds due to his mother's illness, the case was concluded and it was noted that Ramensky (as the prisons still called him) should be transferred to Barlinnie and his girlfriend Miss Mulholland be informed. Lily was also to be told that this was a mere temporary return to Glasgow for Johnny and that his final destination was Peterhead.

For Johnny, there were many years of adventure ahead, playing the same old game with the police and prison authorities. The first of his post-war escapes came eighteen years after that dramatic break from the old jail in 1934. The newspapers of the 1950s were much less constrained than those of the 1930s and the headlines were lurid. There was no end of speculation on how the prisoner – whom the newspapers also still knew as Ramensky – had obtained his freedom. No doubt, too, papers in the central belt, as well as those in the north-east, were getting a circulation boost from covering the story in depth. At this time Johnny had the celebrity that now attaches to pop stars and footballers, if not their wages. Readers followed his exploits on a daily basis with something approaching admiration for his part in the cat and mouse battle being played out. Johnny thought of it all as a game and the press provided regular match reports.

Some remarkable proof of how prominent Johnny was in the public eye came in a book published in 2009 called *Scouting in Banchory*. Written by Michael M. Robson, the book includes many anecdotes from the gang shows that the local Scouts put on, particularly one in the 1950s. Robson writes:

One year during the run of the show the headlines in the Aberdeen *Evening Express* read – 'Johnny Ramensky escapes from Peterhead Jail again!' That night scout Iain Maclennan became Johnny Ramensky and was given an overall suit and cap with arrows painted on them, big boots and a grubby face provided by make-up. Halfway through the evening's entertainment 'Ramensky' crashed through the main Town Hall door just as the compère Captain Duns was about to announce the next item. Iain then raced noisily round the hall a couple of times hotly pursued by a bobby complete with baton.

This little quick-thinking piece of improvised theatre ended with Gentle Johnny escaping backstage and still at liberty. The Ramensky item brought the house down, as they say. The public perception of Johnny is underlined by his description in the book as: 'A noted safecracker but harmless convict and jail-breaker'. Johnny himself may have been on the run that night, not far from where the scouts and their families and friends were enjoying the show. But on or off stage, he was still a bit of a star. And he was held in high affection by the general public if not by his victims.

Early reports of his second Peterhead escape in 1952 reminded those readers who were not aware of it of his service in the Commandos. The blatts of the time appeared to be able to describe his character concisely. One local paper described him as, 'a man of great strength and cunning. Never known to use violence he is capable of feats of endurance even for a few hours of hard-won liberty.'

At the time of this escape Johnny was at odds with the authorities and hassling them for visits south to see his ill mother. The refusals he was getting fuelled his determination to escape. This echoed the escape in 1934, when he was angry and resentful at not being allowed to attend his first wife Daisy's funeral. All his five escapes were partly fuelled by a desire to highlight what he saw as ill treatment or unfairness to himself or his fellow cons. In the later escapes he was well aware of how his celebrity could bring to public attention some of the things he objected to in jail.

In 1952 he was inside, yet again, as a result of being nabbed for blowing open a Post Office safe in Cardonald, Glasgow, not long after his release from the sentence from the York job. When he was sentenced on 20 February 1951, it was said in court that at the end of his war service his discharge certificate read – 'Character exemplary. Honest, reliable man who possesses initiative and a sense of responsibility'. What a shame that when out of the Army Johnny simply could not take to the quiet life. All his positive characteristics were overshadowed by old ways.

How did he get out of jail this time? The Scottish Home Department told the press that for some time he had been employed in 'a semi-trusted job' as an orderly in the prison hospital block. One August night he somehow or other got out of his cell (newspaper stories that he slathered himself with soap and squeezed between a gap in the bars seem too far-fetched to merit consideration) and climbed onto the roof of the prison, then made his way to the yard many feet below.

He was still behind the massive prison wall. But he scaled it, no doubt using some of the rock-climbing techniques he had learned in the Commandos. On the outside, he pinched a girl's bicycle and pedalled off into the dark with the energy of a Chris Hoy. This bike was dumped, but some way from the prison at Glenugie distillery another was stolen. The first bike was taken about 4am and it was an hour later when a lorry driver noticed a man answering the description of Johnny cycling at Longhaven, five miles from Peterhead, in a southerly direction. This was in fact the route taken by Johnny back in 1934.

The police, led by Superintendent Fred Shepard of the North-East Counties force, headquartered in Aberdeen, issued the usual request to all farmers in the Buchan area to search barns, lofts and outhouses for traces of a man on the run. The hunt went much further than this, though. The police were well aware that the famous 'initiative' of the man they called Gentle Johnny made it as likely that he would turn up in Orkney as in the Borders. All police forces throughout Scotland were alerted.

Unlike his previous escape in wintry conditions, this time the weather was warm, dry and clear. More comfortable for an escaper, but not conditions that helped him hide from his pursuers. The farmers and the newspaper readers were in-formed that the convict was wearing a brown moleskin suit with long trousers and a battle-dress type of blouse. He had no headgear but this time he was shod in black shoes and not hobbling along in his bare feet. Newspaper reports pointed out that this escape made Johnny the only man to have escaped from Peterhead twice.

After his first twenty-four hours on the run the newspapers went more in-depth on the escape. The business of getting out of the cell was put down to his ability to pick locks, which was legendary. The cunning lay in his use of a dummy to deceive warders. This was more realistic than the 'soap' theory. His cell had been checked at 7am as part of the daily routine and nothing was seen to be amiss. But the figure lying asleep in the cell was a carefully constructed dummy, cleverly positioned to fool anyone taking a peep into the cell into believing the prisoner was still asleep.

Following this escape Johnny was caught at the very same place where he had been picked up in 1934 – Balmedie, a good number of miles from the prison but only eight from Aberdeen. This time he had been free for forty-seven hours.

The next five years or so were spent quietly in P-head, as it is known in Glasgow crime circles. It was back to the routines of prison life that he was by now so used to. Always a fit man, Johnny loved to play football and work out. He may have had the skills to have become a world famous rock climber but fame in football eluded him.

One man who spent a lot of time in his company in Peterhead in the 1950s was the infamous Glasgow bank robber Walter Norval, a man often described as Glasgow's godfather – the first of several bad guys to lay claim to this title. I tell his story in *Glasgow's Godfather* (Black & White Publishing, Edinburgh, 2011). Norval and Johnny shared an interest in football but they were in a different class on the playing field. Walter remembers that when he was doing a long spell 'up north', football was important to the sanity of men serving sentences that stretched years into the future. This was in the days when remission and curtailed sentences were a distant dream. In prison sport, be it a snooker or pool league or football, is a great safety valve. Energetic young bucks or older fitness fanatics alike could work off their dangerous aggressive tendencies before towelling off the sweat and mud after a hard game.

Walter was a bank robber, who in his heyday was a dangerous man without any of Johnny's distaste for violence and weapons. He was a big figure in prison football circles and a guy who might have made it as pro himself had he not taken so energetically to the life of crime. Indeed when Norval was in borstal, there was talk of him signing for a junior team. But the life he led meant that instead of donning a football shirt and perhaps earning tassled caps and big money, he had to spend many years behind bars following the fortunes of his beloved Celtic in the papers rather than from the terraces. That spell in borstal was a link between the two of them and Walter was always ready to express admiration for Johnny, a man like himself who had survived, and indeed thrived, on a life of crime, despite the pressures of the cruel boot-and-baton regime of the sadistic warders in the old Polmont borstal.

On the football field, the Peterhead cons had a team good enough to take on, and sometimes beat, local minor league teams like Sunnybank, Banks o' Dee, Buckie Thistle and even Peterhead itself. These were the sort of teams that aspired to Hampden and the Junior Cup Final in Glasgow in May, but on occasion they found themselves stretched to beat Walter and his prison mates. The Peterhead cons even saw off a team of superfit young service men from a local air station.

Football was something of a prison religion to the men in Peterhead. The various cellblocks each had teams and played each other in a mini-league. In Walter Norval's time his team, 'B' Block, would usually run out winners and lift the shield that was the prize for the victors. To the desperate convicts it was like winning the Champions League. Poor Johnny was often not even deemed to be skilful enough to play for his hall, never mind the prison team! His only outings were on Sunday afternoons when the wannabes were allowed to play in regular kickabouts. The football committee formed by the prisoners used to pick a couple of sides from the less-skilled and they played each other for the entertainment of the other prisoners and the warders.

Johnny was always at the head of the queue of those waiting to put their names down for one of these kickabouts. These games were billed as 'the Hams v the Bams' matches – no disrespect, just a name picked for a laugh, says Norval. If as a Commando and as a safebreaker Johnny was clearly in the elite, on the football field he was second-class. Though if a ball ended up on the roof there was only one man to retrieve it. Little wonder then that, according to Walter Norval, Johnny spent so many afternoons at the side of the playing field cheering his pals on. Johnny himself liked to tell anyone who would listen that he captained the prison team playing at right back. The prison joke was that the organisers of the Sunday afternoon games had to check Johnny's availability for selection, so often was he outside the wall and on the run!

Willie Leitch, who served many years with Johnny in different jails, confirms Walter Norval's opinion that he was no Puskas. But if his ability as a footballer is doubtful there is no question that his jail pals were in some awe of his skill with the 'devil's pasteboards'. As a card-playing gambler he was in a class of his own.

But for a man of Johnny's restless temperament, football on sunny days and long nights with a sandwich and a cup of tea chatting to the dregs of Glasgow's tough streets were not enough. When his time had been served, Johnny Ramensky was soon looking for the next fix of the drug called excitement and it usually came in the form of another challenging safe. If they said it could not be opened then that made the challenge even more worthwhile. Sadly for Johnny, he never seemed to master evading arrest after his crimes and there was always going to be more jail time coming his way.

# 11

# RECORD-BREAKING
# JAILBREAKER

In the cold of January 1958, Johnny again wrote himself into the record books with his third escape from Peterhead. None of the other thousands of desperate men held in this formidable institution down the years had managed it. The latest jailbreak in the Ramensky series was a little unusual in that he had, for once, the conventional aid of a ladder in scaling the walls. And for the first time tracker dogs were sent after him. The dogs were in no danger from the prisoner for, unlike when he was in Italy, Johnny was not carrying a silenced revolver to use to halt his baying pursuers. Even if he had he would have been unlikely to use it on an animal – he always regretted that incident during the war, even though it had been necessary to ensure the success of a mission.

The dogs on his trail in Scotland belonged to a local couple with an interest in bloodhounds, creatures one normally associates with prison escapes in the Deep South of America rather than rural Aberdeenshire. Straining at the leash, they added a strange touch to a Scottish jailbreak. It is easy to imagine the anger and frustration of police and prison authorities at this escape. The previous breakouts had brought them a monumental amount of negative publicity. The authorities, from governor down to newest recruit in the jail, were not enjoying the jokes doing the rounds in the pubs and clubs of the area. A favourite jibe was to say that if you asked the warders whether Johnny was in the jail any particular day they would have to go and check his cell.

Johnny was now three years into a ten-year stretch handed down by the legendary hammer of the criminal class, Lord Carmont. This time he did not have such a head start on his pursuers as on previous attempts. Only twenty minutes or so. In Peterhead the routine was that the cells were unlocked at around 7.15am. The prisoners' first duty was to clean their cells and generally tidy up. Next they queued in long lines for a meagre breakfast to take back to the cells on a tray. During this period Johnny used the initiative much praised by his Commando chief Lucky Laycock to climb unseen up through a skylight. He then managed to shin up a gas pipe only an inch or two thick and out onto the roof. He was now three storeys up in the bitter cold of a January dawn, but he managed to climb down a rone pipe – a much easier task than scaling a small gas pipe. On the ground he used his lock-breaking skills to get into a shed where he found what he suspected would be there – a ladder, which does indicate rather lax prison security, especially in an institution like Peterhead which was becoming the butt of frequent jokes. Standing the ladder, a pretty short piece of kit, on the top of a shaky bin just barely enabled him to grab the stonework at the top of the eighteen-foot wall. It was then simple for such an experienced and extremely strong climber to hoist himself up and over and away into the dark.

It was thought by the authorities that the escape was a spur-of-the-moment thing rather than a long-planned exploit. Johnny saw an opportunity and took it. And it was almost daylight before he was missed. But as the northern skies slowly lightened, four maltmen at the nearby Glenugie distillery, where work started early, spotted the prisoner making his break. These men were working in the drying barns when in the half-light they saw the dramatic sight of a man fleeing a field opposite the prison and heading for the main road. Johnny was still in the sight of the workers when he reached a cottage near warehouses. They pursued him.

One of the distillery workers, George Henderson, told reporters: 'I think he had a blue jacket and trousers. He walked with his back towards the prison while we kept well behind. He then dodged behind some bushes and disappeared among the warehouses.' Another worker, Sandy Allen, used the patois of the north-east to say that Johnny had 'jouket' the whisky workers then disappeared after jumping over a wall near a shop. This warehouse area was an ideal starting point for the tracker dogs and they quickly picked up the scent of the escaper. But as is often the case with such animals, when they came to the main road, which Johnny had crossed, they became confused by the many other scents from petrol fumes and other pedestrians and completely lost the trail.

One of the first places searched was Dales Home Farm, about three quarters of a mile from the jail. The daughter of the grieve, an eight-year-old called Gladys Krowcyk, was looking out of a window just before eight o'clock and saw a man she did not recognise running past, just a few yards from where she watched. But she did not mention it to her mother until some time later. Various false alarms were raised including 'sightings' in Stonehaven and Laurencekirk.

This escape provoked a huge escalation in the hunt for Johnny compared with what had happened in the past. Police were deployed in large numbers to all parts of Aberdeenshire, Banff and Kincardine. The usual time-consuming and labour-intensive tactic of searching dozens of barns and empty farm buildings was again in progress in the belief that Johnny would lie low in daytime and only travel by night. The warders who had been assigned to help the police even went to the length of sticking hayforks into rigs in case the wily escaper was having a quiet kip under warm straw – something he had been known to do. The police also called for the public to report the theft of bikes, cars or motorbikes, even milk bottles.

The day of the escape was market day in Aberdeen itself and farmers and their animals travelling to this notable event were delayed at numerous checkpoints causing great confusion in the city and its suburbs. At one checkpoint, Bridge of Don, hundreds of folk were stopped. Mind you, it would all give the farmers and their employees something different to talk about in the many pubs thronged with drouthy visitors to the market. For once the talk in the howffs was about more than the price fetched by one prized animal or another.

So high-profile were the escape and the manhunt that it is no surprise Johnny was nabbed pretty quickly. The whole population of north-eastern Scotland was on the lookout for the serial escaper – and they all knew from the papers, and the stories of his wartime bravery, what he looked like. His notoriety was such that on the run he might as well have worn a tag round his neck announcing, 'I am Ramensky'. He was not going to disappear unrecognised into a crowd. Without an accomplice and without transport or ready access to food it was inevitable he would soon be recaptured. But in this, the third of his five escapes from Peterhead, he managed to stay free for twenty-eight hours.

He was 'collared' on the streets of Peterhead, despite being disguised as a warder and wearing a blue regulation coat and cheese-cutter cap, items he had stolen from a shed near the prison. He had spent the previous night hiding audaciously on the roof of a local school, calmly watching the search parties below bent on hunting him down. It must have brought back memories of hiding in Italy with his partisan comrades. It was another satisfying little adventure, a memorable moment in the game of cops and robbers he played all his life.

His fourth escape saw him wandering Aberdeenshire for a little longer – forty hours. He escaped on a Friday night and was caught on the Sunday, just a few hundred yards from the jail. He had got lucky during his previous escape when little Gladys Krowcyk had waited for an hour or so before telling her mother about the mystery man she had seen outside the window that January day. But this time his downfall was a seven-year-old boy. And the old 'search the hayloft' ploy paid off.

Wee David Smith lived on his father's farm at Meethill, Peterhead, and on the Sunday morning he had gone with George Henderson, a casual worker on the farm, to the hayloft. David, a bright youngster, told his companion, 'Someone has been shifting the bales' and then he climbed into them and shouted, 'Ramensky is here.' Such was Johnny's fame that even a seven-year-old boy recognised him and knew his name immediately.

Wee David later said: 'I saw Ramensky lying among the bales of straw. He said to me: "You should not have come in here, sonny." I shouted to Mr Henderson. I was a bit frightened. But Ramensky said, "Don't be scared, sonny. I won't hurt you."'

George Henderson kept an eye on Johnny as wee David ran to summon his father. When they were all outside the loft, David's dad and Mr Henderson tried to persuade Johnny to give himself up and offered to drive him to the prison in the farm truck. 'Nothing doing,' said Johnny. 'Just give me a five-minute start and they won't catch me.' It was something of a pathetic scene, with Johnny pleading for his freedom in front of a child.

Farmer Smith commented on how old and decrepit the man on the run looked and remarked that they could not bring themselves to use force on him. It was a prescient observation and an early sign that the years were beginning to catch up with Johnny. Mr Smith told reporters: 'He looked a lot more than his fifty-three years. One foot was bare and bleeding. He had a piece of dirty bandage tied round it, but it could not have been doing much good.' The escaper then started away from the farm along a country track and George Henderson stayed with him while farmer Smith drove to the prison for assistance. Henderson must have had good reason to be fed up with Ramensky and his jailbreaks – this is the same George Henderson who, when working at the distillery, trailed him on break number three!

As they walked along, he tried to talk Johnny into seeing sense and returning to the prison for food and treatment for his injuries. But the escaper was determined to carry on, however hopeless it looked. When the two of them reached a spot near the distillery, the police were already there. Johnny made one last attempt at avoiding them by lying down behind a dyke. But when he saw Inspector John Campbell and a Constable Hendry he finally accepted that the game was up and walked towards them.

It was a sad scene. He was wearing an old, long, checked overcoat, presumably stolen from some place, and George Henderson said: 'Ramensky must have been chilled to the bone. He was clutching the coat about him and looked very old. He did not say much when he was walking along with me. He just asked me to leave him alone.'

The miserable escaper was taken to Peterhead police HQ, where he got a change of clothing and a hot meal. Another court appearance beckoned in Aberdeen, where he would be sentenced for the jailbreak, adding more time to a huge number of years spent behind bars. There was another spectacular break to come but this, his fourth time over the wall, made him once again Scotland's top jailbreaker. This was something in which he took pride. His record had been dented up to this time by a prisoner called John Burnside who had escaped from a Scottish jail five times, but 'only' three times from Peterhead which was considered the nearest thing to Alcatraz to be found in Scotland.

Police mug shots of Scotland's most famous safecracker – with and without his trademark soft hat.

## Military History Sheet.

Service at Home and Abroad.

| Country. | Service to count as British or Indian. | From | To | Length of Service. | |
|---|---|---|---|---|---|
| | | | | Years. | Days. |
| HOME | BRITISH. | 19·1·43 | 24.3.44. | 1 | 66 |
| N.AFRICA | | 25.3.44 | 12-8-45 | 1 | 141 |
| Home | | 13-8-45 | 23.2.46 | | 195 |
| BAOR | | 24.2.46 | 25.6.46. | – | 122 |
| Home. | | 26.6.46 | 10·9·46 | | 77 |
| Class 2 (T) Res | | 11.9.46 | 10 FEB 1954 | | |

N.B.—The Country only to be shewn.—It is not necessary to shew separately the service in the different stations of the same country. England, Scotland and Ireland to be shewn under the general term "Home."

For mode of computing service abroad see King's Regulations.

*Note.*—Service reckoning as Indian Service to be inserted in Red Ink.

21771 Wt. 32606/1838 1,000,000 11/30 MsC & Co—T 5259. Forms/B200a/18

A simple piece of Army paperwork – but behind this understated bureaucratic record is one of the most remarkable stories in the history of the Second World War.

| Enlisted at | Glasgow | | on 19·1·43 | |
|---|---|---|---|---|
| Nature of Engagement (including variations in terms of service after enlistment). | Corps or Regiment. | Service towards limited engagement reckons from | Former service in the | |

| | | | | Allowed to reckon as :— |
|---|---|---|---|---|
| **DOW** | **THE ROYAL FUSILIERS.** | 19 · 1 · 43 | | "Service." Years Days |
| | | | | "Qualifying Service." Years Days |

| No. of Part II Order or other Authority. | Unit. | Promotions, Reductions, Casualties, CONTINUED FROM ARMY FORM E. 531 | Army Rank. | Dates. | Service not allowed to reckon for fixing rate of pension. Years. Days. | Authenticating Signature or Initials. |
|---|---|---|---|---|---|---|
| | Commando Depot | Posted | Fus. | 19·1·43 91/45×L.C.M.F. | | |
| | | [boxes] 1463 / 1 263 To:- / 32 | **C** | 5.4.'45 | | |
| 233/45 CMF | X LIST | Awarded 8 days C.B. for (1) AWOL 2359 hrs 27·7·45 to 0035 hrs 28·7·45 (2) Being out after curfew on 27·7·45 | Fus. | 16·7·45 | | |
| | | Proceeded on Terminal Leave War Gratuity Rank 01634C To R·P | Fus. (Fus) · | 28·6·46 28·6·46 | | |
| | | RELEASED TO CLASS 'Z' (T) ARMY RESERVE DATE 11 September 46 (CLASS 'A' RELEASE) | | | | W E Edwards Lt Co INF & APTC RECORDS ASHFORD, MIDDX. RECORD OFFICER |
| | | "Discharged para 234-1 T.A. Regs. 1952, on termination of engagement" ATTAINS AGE of 45 No further LIABILITY FOR RECALL | | 10 FEB 1953 | Total | |

| Total Service towards Engagement to ............... (date of discharge) ............... Years ............ Days. | | | | | | |
|---|---|---|---|---|---|---|
| "    "    "    Pension "    "    " | | | | Years ............ Days. | | |

2866500

More Army paperwork including a reference to a little episode that saw him confined to barracks after a short spell AWOL

# COMMANDO
## SERVICE CERTIFICATE

Italy       Crete       Burma       Greece
Norway      France      Sicily      Albania
Holland     Belgium     Germany     Madagascar
North Africa Yugoslavia Western Desert Channel Islands

This Certificate is an Appreciation,
of Loyal Service given to Commandos by

R. Laycock.
Chief of Combined Operations

Served in Commando's until November 1945.

8th November 1945

A certificate of appreciation signed by the famous "Lucky"
Laycock, Chief of Combined Operations.

The most spectacular of the mementoes acquired by Johnny in Germany and
Italy are a pair of Nazi banners complete with swastikas and heavy gold trim,
one reading Marshall of the Great German Empire, the other, Commander-
in-Chief of the Luftwaffe. Also securely held in the safety of a Scottish bank
are his well-used green beret and other bits and pieces from his life behind the
lines, including a trusty Commando compass and a silk handkerchief map.

© MIRRORPIX.COM

Johnny's wedding to Lily in 1955 – the marriage was punctuated with separations caused by his convictions and banishment to what Lily called his "second home" – prison. Also in the bridal party are Lily's son Jim and daughter Maureen.

© HERALD AND TIMES GROUP

Ramensky enjoys the comfort of an armchair and a wee glance at a newspaper at his home in Eglinton Street in Glasgow.

© MIRRORPIX.COM

Johnny's life was lived in headlines; throughout his career the tabloids in particular featured him regularly. This typical front page shows an excellent shot of him on recapture after one of the three escapes he made from Peterhead in 1958. The tiredness and resignation is clear.

Johnny enjoying freedom in his usual smart dress, the overcoat expensive, the shoes shined. Window shopping was a pleasure when not behind bars.

Johnny Beattie, a Glasgow theatrical legend, met Johnny and Lily backstage when they came to see him play the Ayr Gaiety and found them a likeable and surprisingly "ordinary" couple.

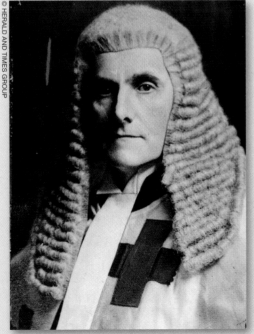

After the Second World War, Lord Carmont worked to quell a crime wave that swept Glasgow. He cracked down hard on those like the razor slashers whose antics blackened the city – but he also showed no mercy to Johnny who appeared before him on safe blowing charges.

With a smile and his few belongings in a battered little suitcase, Johnny heads for a wee holiday down the coast. There is optimism in his face that suggests he believed, as usual on a release, that his prison days were behind him for good. But he never managed to go straight for lengthy periods.

The flamboyant Nicky Fairbairn, and Joe Beltrami, aka "The Great Defender", just two of the many lawyers who fought to keep Johnny out of jail. But usually there was just too much evidence against the safecracker.

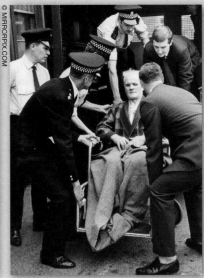

A reflective moment of freedom on a beach. There were few such open-air breaks for a man who spent the majority of his life looking out from behind prison bars and doing more "porridge" than even the most infamous of killers, despite his own abhorrence of violence.

In a wheelchair for a court appearance after his fall from a roof during one of his last jobs in the early seventies. Severely injured in an attempt to escape the police he was never again the lithe, super-fit gymnastic cat-burglar of his early years.

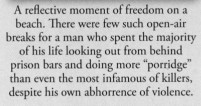

An iconic picture of prisoners on the roof at Barlinnie. But the antics of these protestors was not unique. Back in the early thirties Ramensky scaled a rone pipe leading to the roof tops of the prison. He stayed up for several hours, walking the high ridge, throwing slates at the warders below and asking for some hard boiled eggs to be hurled up to him. Hunger eventually made him give up his spectacular display, a protest at the way he was being treated.

The Commando memorial at Spean Bridge is one of Scotland's most spectacular sculptures. It brilliantly conveys the spirit of the brave men who trained in the snows of Lochaber before being parachuted into Europe's war zones to help fight and defeat the menace of German fascism.

Johnny's great granddaughter Kendal Ferguson visits his grave in Lambhill, Glasgow. Kendal is a keen student of Johnny's Army career.

UNITED · WE · CONQUER

IN·MEMORY·OF
THE·OFFICERS·AND
MEN·OF
THE·COMMANDOS
WHO·DIED·IN·THE
SECOND·WORLD·WAR
1939-1945
THIS·COUNTRY·WAS
THEIR·TRAINING
GROUND

# 12

# A BAR-L BREAK-IN
# FOR A CHANGE ...

Connoisseurs of the art of jailbreaking would probably say that the daddy of Johnny's five escapes from Peterhead was the last, at Christmas 1958. This put him in a class of his own as an escaper. He was recaptured near Aberdeen, but he had been free for a couple of hours short of nine days. Some going, particularly considering his celebrity.

There is a real mystery about this jailbreak. It does not at all follow the pattern of his previous escapes. To stay free for such a time needs more than good luck and Commando training. Somewhere along the line you need help. And if you turn up and are recaptured not looking old and decrepit – as in the previous escape – but clean-shaven, well fed and chipper, then the suspicion has to be that Ramensky had help – a lot of help.

Did he get shelter and food from some kind-hearted but 'misguided' local, as one paper put it? That seems likely. But one ex-con who knew him well thought he did it on his own, living off the country and using some of his Commando expertise. He advised that Johnny was even expert at guddling a trout when hungry. But the clean-shaven bit does seem to be a clincher for the theory that he had help.

Johnny would not tell the authorities whether or not he had had any assistance in staying free for so many days. He was keeping this a secret for his memoirs, he remarked with a smile. You must presume, too, that he was protecting the person who had assisted him. There are some in the area today who believe that on this occasion he was sheltered by a kindly elderly lady enamoured of his reputation as Gentle Johnny.

Oddly enough the Balmedie district featured again in his getaway. At daybreak on his ninth day out of the jail a lorry driver saw him. Such was the headline furore about this final hunt for Johnny that the driver was in no doubt who he had spotted. Again the public's knowledge of his appearance had aided his downfall. The actual location of this sighting was not far away from Menie, where he had been recaptured in 1934 and 1952.

Perhaps emboldened by his success in staying free so long, Johnny had actually asked the lorry driver for a lift. The driver said no, but as he drove off, Johnny jumped into the back of the lorry with typical deftness, but jumped out again when the driver stopped to check his load. The driver, however, was a former Peterhead warder and he carried on to Aberdeen to tell the police there about his unwanted passenger. Johnny must have been getting careless by this time for a bus driver also spotted him walking on the main road near Mandurno. And workers at a sandpit in the area also told the police they had seen him, crossing fields from Carnfield farm to Buckie farm and heading in the direction of Persley. One of the youths at the sandpit, Eddie White, said: 'I kent he was a stranger from the way he was walking. He looked a bit lost. When I got closer I recognised him but I waited till he was alongside to make sure. I said, "Fine day." He didn't catch what I said and said, "Eh?" I repeated, "It's a fine day" and he said, "Oh aye" and continued on his way.'

A young RAF man home on leave and staying at Buckie farm saw Johnny crossing the field and phoned the police from the farmhouse. He told the cops the fugitive looked remarkably fit and was wearing clean blue denims. This led to a search party spotting him and after an abortive attempt to run away Johnny gave up quietly. A senior police officer said he seemed in good fettle and only his cracked and burst shoes gave evidence of a man on the run. It seems obvious that he had been hidden by someone, perhaps no surprise given his fame in the north-east and the mutual affection between Johnny and the folk of the area.

It is perhaps hard now, in these times of gun and knife-toting gangsters, to understand just how the public perceived Johnny in the Peterhead area. His attitude of 'going quietly' made him many friends. Remember the genuine affection shown to him at that Gang Show. And it should not be forgotten that the people of the area were familiar with prisoners out in the fields with work parties. Also, some of the local men would work as warders in the prison and share leisure time at football matches with the convicts. Added to that, Johnny was a genuine legend inside the jail itself.

Back in Peterhead, Johnny was not the only man in trouble. Governor Duncan Mackenzie, who ruled the prison from 1958 to 1961 and who also had a spell in charge of Barlinnie, was also in some hot water. The daring and audacity of the Ramsay escapes may have made him something of a star with the public – at court appearances of this time, crowds chanting 'Good old Johnny' were a regular sight. But Duncan Mackenzie's bosses in Edinburgh took a dim view. Days after the last escape, the governor was summoned to St Andrew's House in Edinburgh and given a wigging. It was pointed out that Johnny was making the prison a laughing stock. He was not to be allowed to escape again. Full stop!

The simplest way to see that did not happen was to put him under a 24/7 watch. Six officers were specially selected to watch over his movements in the prison, twenty-four hours a day, seven days a week. The old rebel did not like this one bit and muttered on and on about how he would still make a break for it if he felt like it. But eventually even he realised the impossibility of escape under such surveillance and abandoned the idea. Duncan Mackenzie, the quietly spoken son of a Highland crofter, was wise in the ways of the prison service and despite the trouble Johnny had caused him he developed an admiration for him and a desire to help him change his ways.

Johnny served time under three governors of Peterhead and had a mixed relationship with the other two – Captain J. I. Buchan and Major D. C. Heron-Watson. It is little wonder they did not subscribe to the usual 'likeable rogue' description – for them he spelled constant trouble with his escapes and his jailhouse lawyer habits. There were some acts of kindness though, in amongst the harsher treatment. For example, Governor Heron-Watson showed him some kindness by allowing him to keep a diary, although this act of seeming generosity later brought the Governor a rap over the knuckles from Edinburgh. And, of course, Buchan played a major role in getting him into the Army.

His troubles with governors apart, Johnny's legendary like-ability extended to young and old alike. He simply just got along with people. John Mathers is a retired builder now living in North Berwick, but when he was boy of eleven or so he had an interesting encounter with the safecracker. John lived at South Kirkton farm on the Fraserburgh to Peterhead road, just a few miles or so from the jail. In the summer, work parties from the jail were a regular sight in the fields of Kirkton and other farms in the area. As a wee boy John crept out after school to watch these convict workers, who toiled all day, harvesting among the stooks. He was not scared of the cons. And he remembers how Johnny's disposition shone through. Even to such a youngster it was obvious that the guy in charge of the party of seven or eight prisoners at South Kirkton was Johnny Ramensky, not the prison officer who was with them.

Johnny was a natural organiser and it showed. He took a liking to the lad who watched them work and made a deal with him: if he gathered any old cigarette ends lying around the streets or fields and collected them in a box and handed them over to Johnny he would get a wee reward. Johnny had wangled himself the easiest job working in the fields, naturally, driving the tractor. And young John's reward for collecting snout – that most valuable commodity in any prison – was to get a wee shot of driving.

Young John Mathers duly handed over boxes of fag ends dredged from the roadside and gutters and Johnny kept his part of the deal – the lad was allowed to drive the tractor. After the handover of the tobacco there was a ritual that fascinated wee John and maybe showed the prisoner's mastery of fire and fuse that owed much to his ability with explosives. The safe blower had a wee tinderbox and used a piece of steel and a flint to spark a light to some loose cotton in the box. On these occasions the tinderbox was used simply to light a roll-your-own cigarette, but it could have worked to get a fuse going as well!

This story surprised Johnny's niece Dorothy when she heard the details. She thinks Johnny was mostly a non-smoker. So maybe these cigarettes were intended to go back into the jail as 'currency' to be sold to other cons and give Johnny a little extra cash for wee treats, as he called them.

Life in rural Aberdeenshire in the 1940s and 1950s had its own dangers. John Mathers recalls taking the bus into Peterhead to attend the Boys' Brigade and returning to walk up a pitch-dark track to the house on a cloudy night. He still remembers one occasion when he was sure that someone was hiding in the bushes at the side of the track. He did not investigate but hurried to the welcoming light of the farmhouse in the distance. In the morning his father, a shepherd, told him that there had indeed been an escape from the jail the previous night. Was wee John's pal with the magic tinderbox hiding in the bushes?

Another man with memories of Johnny during that era is Charles Gordon, who retired as Sheriff Clerk at the county of Banff in May 1981. Charles Gordon was Sheriff Clerk Depute at Aberdeen Sheriff Court on a day when Johnny was charged with 'prisonbreaking'. He vividly remembers the strikingly 'innocent appearance' of the prisoner. According to the veteran court official, a man who ran countless trials and saw thousands of criminals in the dock, Johnny simply did not look the sort of man you would expect to be involved in crime. He had the same impression of the man as hundreds of others who met him and were surprised by his kindly appearance. Maybe this disposition played a role in creating his nickname, as well as his genuine non-violent attitude to a life of crime.

It is interesting, too, that Mr Gordon remembers that the spelling of Ramensky in the court proceedings was Ramenski. This was years after the official name change to Ramsay. But confusion over the various versions of Johnny's name continued down the years. I have seen documents written by Johnny himself while in Perth Prison and they clearly show him using the form 'Ramensky' rather than the Ramsay you would expect after his war service was over.

As this particular trial was about to start, Charles Gordon bumped into a famous procurator fiscal of the north-east, a Mr Mill, and asked him if he expected a conviction. The lawyer pooh-poohed as naive any suggestion that there was any other possible verdict than guilty. But Charles Gordon knew better than anyone how Johnny's non-violent reputation and the high regard he was held in by the Scottish public could affect a jury. No one can offer a better guess at any trial to the likely response from the jury than the clerk. Wise court lawyers heed their counsel. The verdict was, of course, in the end, guilty – after all, no one could deny Johnny had somehow managed to scale the prison walls and go on the run for days. But the jury's verdict was not unanimous and this, in Charles Gordon's opinion, showed the reluctance of some, at least, of the north-east jurors to side with the law against the folk hero. Proof again that Johnny was a sort of modern version of Robin Hood in the eyes of some who followed his career and noted his reputation of specialising in robbing businesses rather than private homes.

Charles Gordon, now almost in his nineties, remembers hearing in court how the prisoners were counted out for exercise but mysteriously one prisoner was missing as they were counted in. This counting them out and counting them in was a particularly wise procedure since Johnny had escaped so often from Scotland's toughest jail. Nothing new was revealed in this particular trial about how he got over the wall or how he survived outside. But his escape had sparked some astonishing rumours. One senior police officer in all seriousness told Charles Gordon that he believed the elusive safecracker had been picked up from a North Sea beach and spirited away in a submarine. Some who believed this tale thought that it all had something to do with a film.

One interesting wee story did emerge about Johnny's capture. Offered tea, he declined. And he informed his captors that he was not hungry, though by then it was almost lunchtime. As previously noted, his clean-shaven appearance, commented on in the newspapers, was a million miles from what you expect of a con on the run. Proof, suggests Charles Gordon, that a member of the public had indeed harboured Johnny, as many believed. Long after that trial for escaping, one famous sheriff told Charles Gordon that had Ramensky appeared before him accused of a jailbreak he would have liked to have found a way round the law to admonish him! However this break did cost Johnny further time in jail. He was punished by having eighteen months added to his sentence, though on appeal that was reduced to a year.

It seems fitting to end this account of Johnny's jailbreaks with a report on his involvement in an attempt to break *in* to jail! The story is tucked away in Scotland's National Archives in

Charlotte Square in Edinburgh, and is an amazing and little-known piece of Barlinnie prison history.

It happened on the night of 10 February 1951, when Johnny was temporarily in the Bar-L, rather than Peterhead, perhaps back in Glasgow to have visits from friends, relatives or whatever. This remarkable incident is recorded in some detail in a report written for the governor by a Barlinnie prison officer called Thompson. It told of an escapade that raised eyebrows and caused a little wry amusement when it was forwarded to the prison service authorities in Edinburgh.

Officer Thompson recorded that the outside patrol officer was taken aback on his round – usually a cushy bit of work since the prison was so hard to break out of. The normally uneventful evening stroll round the outside of the dark, high walls, was livened up when, around 9pm, the patrolling officer spotted someone trying to attach a hook from the outside of the prison onto the top of the south-west corner of the huge perimeter wall. Three officers were immediately despatched to the scene and another two deployed inside the prison in the area where the hook was being fastened.

The guy on the outside was quickly recognised by the officers as an ex-prisoner, Daniel Hynds. It was ascertained equally swiftly that he had visited the prison earlier in the day. The man he went to see was none other than Johnny Ramensky. When they met they must have passed more than the time of day. An officer was despatched into the yard under the outside window of Johnny's cell and when Hynds arrived there he whistled loudly. A hand appeared at a ventilator but soon disappeared and when officers inside the prison went to Ramensky's cell he had craftily returned to bed. Whatever was going on, a break in or out or whatever, the plan had been foiled.

The report found its way to the highly polished wooden desks of the bigwigs in the Scottish Office and memos flew on the subject of break-ins. Surprisingly one noted, 'It is understood Edinburgh is vulnerable and that "nocturnal two-way traffic is not unheard of in Perth Prison" but this seems to be the first time an attempt has been made to break in to Barlinnie.' A senior civil servant had scrawled in ink under this report 'Interesting!' Indeed. Gentle Johnny Ramensky had been involved in another piece of prison history.

# 13

# ROUGH JUSTICE

The last two decades of Johnny's life were a strange mixture of short periods of domestic happiness, when not behind bars; even shorter periods of excitement, when on the run after a jailbreak; and mind-bendingly dull years of extended confinement.

In his jailbreaking career, he set the bar high for any subsequent career criminals bent on beating his record. Old lags will tell you that the modern inclination to hand jail transfers and other aspects of the prison service to private firms makes 'doing a runner' much easier than in the old days. These days the papers are peppered with stories of criminals who abscond at court appearances and other weak points in the new privatised system. These escapes are usually short-lived. But just as old time bank robbers and godfathers regard some of today's criminal classes dismissively as 'gas meter bandits', jailbreaks in which the prisoner scales high walls and swings hand over hand under bridges guarded by road blocks at each end, are now few and far between.

In Johnny's case, the necessity to escape in the first place was an obvious result of his reluctance to go straight – despite the pleas and offers of assistance from the many friends he had made down the years. In the 1950s and 1960s there may have been many long years of boredom behind bars, but some of the escapades that led to the jail terms were as exciting as any of his adventures in the Commandos. And they also demonstrate that the legend of 'Gentle Johnny' and his persistent stoic acceptance of his fate, when caught, are generally true. There were occasions when he did not go quite as quietly as the legend would have it – but on each of those occasions, when he breached his own rules, there were, as they say in the courts, extenuating circumstances.

Two defining trials in Ramensky's life of crime occurred in 1955 and in 1967. Both crimes were committed in the Southside of Glasgow, Johnny's home patch. His own fireside was usually in Eglinton Street, just across the Clyde from the city centre, but he was still spending time in Rutherglen with his sisters Agnes and Margaret and his niece Dorothy. In the first of these crimes he proved he could be remarkably restrained in trying circumstances, but in the second his fists came into play.

The first incident occurred during the raid on a garage. A retired police officer, William Johnston, now living in the pleasant Southside suburb of Cathcart, recalled it in some detail. He had just come out of police training college and was on beat patrol in Croftfoot, near the huge post-war housing scheme of Castlemilk. Close to what is now known as the Croftfoot roundabout, there was the sort of local garage very common in the days before the major manufacturers took over servicing and sales. This was a good-going old-fashioned garage, with a healthy customer base of middle-class folk having their cars serviced monthly or at 1,000-mile intervals, whichever came first, as the handbooks of those far-off days recommended.

In the 1950s, a garage tended to have a safe that would be well stocked after a busy day of minor repairs on cars that, unlike today's 'unplug and replace' vehicles, could actually be worked on by real mechanics. Maybe Johnny had noticed the busy place going back and forward to family in the nearby 'Mulk' as it was known, or perhaps on jaunts from his sister's house in Rutherglen, not too far away. The garage – now replaced by a supermarket – faced the main road coming down the hill from

Castlemilk towards Mount Florida and Hampden Park. It had some obvious attractions for a safecracker other than its apparently good financial health. At the back of the place it was pretty quiet, shielded from the traffic on the main road. At one side of the street at the back there was the quietness of King's Park, a pleasant place for Croftfoot folk to relax in daylight hours. At night no one ventured over the high iron fences other than the odd teenage couple on the lookout for a little hanky panky underneath the rhododendrons. On the other side of the street, some distance from the garage, there was a row of douce four-in-a-block houses.

A break-in at this site must have been appealing to Johnny. It seemed an easy touch to a man of his experience. But this time he got a little careless – his entry through a skylight or back window, Mr Johnston is not sure which, was heralded by the sound of breaking glass. Not the usual modus operandi of the master cracksman creeping silently across the roof tiles. Something had gone wrong. You might think that after this a prudent burglar would have fled the scene. Not Johnny – that safe was there to be opened. But this time the expert safecracker had made enough noise to alert an elderly woman in one of the houses near the garage. She phoned the cops and a squad car and some beat men arrived soon arrived.

One of the beat coppers, John Lawrie, drew his baton and entered the darkened building. He whacked the intruder, who had given away his location with a movement in the dark. Johnny was not seriously injured, though he could have been, but he had to be taken to the nearby Victoria Infirmary for a stitch or two. He was far from happy at this attack on him, but he did not respond with violence. Indeed, officers at the scene of his arrest on this occasion thought his attitude verged on the timid and they reported he was certainly non-aggressive.

In this instance, the seemingly harsh response of whacking Gentle Johnny with a baton was controversial and John Lawrie took some criticism from the public for his action when it was reported in the press. But as his colleague William Johnston points out, when Lawrie drew the baton and entered the garage he did not know whether he faced an unarmed man or two or three villains, perhaps with guns or knives. It is a constant dilemma for a man on the beat and most elect to take no chances and swing a baton. Whatever, Johnny was back behind bars and he took exception that a cop had thumped him first and asked questions afterwards. He seemed almost affronted that a policeman had seen fit to hit him. No doubt he felt that PC Lawrie should have known of his reputation for going quietly!

The old lady who had called the cops got a commendation from the chief constable and Johnny's reputation for non-violence was given a little more burnishing. However, his ego was dented, both when the mistake he had made when breaking in and by meeting a cop who had used a baton against him.

Incidentally, William Johnston remembers meeting Johnny on another occasion in Eglinton Street, when an older partner on the beat pointed him out to the tyro cop. His main memory of the meeting is that Johnny looked dapper in his usual suit and trademark smart soft hat amidst the undoubtedly somewhat time-worn surroundings of the old Eglinton Street tenements. To the cops he was a man of significance, well worth watching, and to the locals a legend to be pointed out.

The court appearance following this escapade marked a change in style for Johnny. It was perhaps the final turning point in his career, the moment when he at last realised and admitted to himself that there was no hope of going straight. As we have seen, for years he had indulged himself as a jailhouse lawyer, helping his fellow convicts when, as he saw it, they got a rough deal. And he had had a bit of success in making life a little easier behind bars for his pals from time to time. No doubt his skill in writing letters, on behalf of both others and himself, gave him a notion that he could do better than some of the defence lawyers who had made money representing him. And maybe he had a point, for defence counsels never seemed to have much success keeping him out of jail – or even keeping his sentences short. In fact, a study of his numerous court appearances shows that his Gentle Johnny approach never did him much good when in the dock. 'Likeable rogue' or not, he was still dealt some harsh judgements from the bench. This seems to underline the belief, often mentioned by old lags, that justice at times looked more harshly at crimes against business than crimes of violence.

When he appeared in Glasgow High Court in November 1955 he admitted that he had 'broken into Croftfoot Garage, Carmunnock Road, Glasgow and by means of explosives forced open a lock fast safe and stolen cash'. But this time he decided to discard help from his counsel and make his own plea for leniency. Here was more great headline fodder for the city's papers. It was not as sensational as Peter Manuel's appropriation a few years later of a fantasy legal gown and his sacking of a well-known QC in a failed fight to save his neck from the hangman. But it was pretty dramatic all the same, as the war hero pleaded for yet another last chance.

Johnny Ramensky clearly realised that he had to pull out all the stops if his sentence wasn't going to be very severe indeed. He knew he could elicit sympathy from a jury, and perhaps even from some judges, but for obvious reasons he had decided to plead guilty and the only man who now mattered was the man on the bench – in this case the formidable and legendary Lord Carmont. And he was no soft touch for a sob story.

At this time, Carmont was engaged in a war against the city's infamous razor slashers and intent on ending the post-war surge in crime. He had the support of the city's newspaper leader writers, who liked his merciless approach. In private life, Carmont was a kind and generous man, but in court he was as hard as nails. His belief was that the cure to the crime wave of the time was long sentences. He was convinced that the only way to stop frequent offenders was to get them off the streets for fearsomely long stretches in Scotland's toughest jails and he wanted to instil a fear of offending into the criminal classes. Such was the severity of his sentencing policy that sixty or so years later you will still hear criminals calling a long sentence 'doing a Carmont', though by now they may have no idea who he was.

Before listening to Johnny's plea for mercy, Lord Carmont asked the accused if he had been offered the services of counsel. Johnny said he had but that he pleaded guilty and wished to speak for himself. The advocate depute, Mr V. Skae, offered some words of mitigation and he told his lordship it might be said that, 'Ramsay had tendered considerable assistance to the War Department during the late war through his specialised knowledge of safe breaking.' Clearly this line of defence was wearing a little thin as Mr Skae added: 'But, I feel bound to say that this was taken into account at the last time he was before the court on a similar charge.'

Lord Carmont then asked the advocate depute to detail Johnny's previous court appearances. It was quite a list, beginning with an appearance for theft in 1916 (when he was eleven) at which he was admonished. After this came a Sheriff Court appearance when he was ordered to be detained in borstal for three years. He was back in the dock in 1924 when he got three years' hard labour. Next came his first High Court appearance on a series of housebreaking charges and, interestingly, one of assault. In 1927 he got three years. In 1932 came the first charge involving explosives and other court appearances came in 1934, 1938, 1947 and 1951.

Lord Carmont listened to it all carefully and turned to Johnny in the dock, using the name Ramensky rather than Ramsay, and said: 'You have heard what has been read out as your past record. What have you to say before I deal with your plea of guilty to this present charge?'

In contemporary reports, Ramensky was described as 'an alert figure with his fair hair going grey'. He answered rather hesitantly that he was 'very sorry for what I have done'. He was at this time shuffling from foot to foot in the dock and to onlookers appeared to be groping for words. Carmont was about to proceed but his attention was drawn to the fact that the accused appeared not to be finished.

'Go on, say what you have to say,' said the great judge.

It was quite a lot. Johnny got out the specs and a wad of notes.

'My Lord,' he said, ' I am very sorry for what I have done and the trouble I have caused. It can never happen again. All the money in the world could never compensate for the misery and suffering I have brought to my wife through my fault. This is my constant reproach. I committed this offence in a mood of anger because I had lost all my money at dog tracks. When a man is angry he is unreasonable and he commits acts which he later regrets. Such was my condition at the time of the offence and I appeal to you, My Lord, for a chance. A chance I never had. I do not ask for a chance just because I never had it but because I promise sincerely that this is my last appearance in court.'

He then went on to give the judge an account of his early life.

'My life,' he said, 'has been rather grim and all because I started off on the wrong foot. I was only seven when my father died and I moved from Glenboig to Glasgow. We lived in the slums where the city urchins soon led me into crime and trouble. My troubles mounted and at the age of twenty I appeared at the High Court and was sentenced to eighteen months for housebreaking. I am now fifty years old and I have spent thirty of them in prison – thirty years of misery and privation. The average sentence served by a reprieved murderer is ten years. So I have already served three life sentences for my misdeeds in the past. The law has had more than its pound of flesh. Would it be wrong for me to ask for a chance now? If I had been shown a little kindness in the past, my life would have been different today.

'During my last sentence I wrote my life story – 250,000 words of it. I was granted interviews with newspapermen who promised me thousands for my story. I was happy and contented at the prospect and looked forward to a new life.

'But the day before my release I was called before the governor of Barlinnie prison and he told me my book was impounded and by the Secretary of State [John Stuart], my story suppressed and that the manuscripts would be destroyed three months from the date of my liberation.'

For the first time in his statement Johnny raised his voice:

'That was unfair to me as the authorities had built up my mind for four years. On the next day, when I was liberated, I was met by newspapermen who took me to London but when the editors learned that my book was impounded they lost their interest. Eventually one paper printed a few articles and paid me a fair sum. With this sum I got married in February [the trial was in November] to the dearest and sweetest woman in the world. For her sake I ask for a chance to prove to her that I am not really bad and that I can live an honest life. Surely it is not too late for that. I have tried hard to live an honest life and for eight months I did well. If I had not yielded to a fit of temper I would still have been a free and happy man – and I was happy after years of misery and hardship. I have found in my marriage what real happiness meant. Give me a chance, My Lord, to cement our happiness.'

Still consulting the papers in his hand, he moved on to detail his war record.

'During the last war I was tested and I was not found wanting. I joined the Commandos straight from prison in 1942. I was invited to Whitehall to meet the chiefs of the Commandos who made me a proposition. I accepted it gladly and promised to play my part. For three and a half years I served in the Commandos with honour and distinction and in 1946 I was demobilised with an honourable discharge and letters of merit from various Army chiefs. I made my promise to the Commandos and I kept it. I only mention this to show that I can keep a promise if I make one. I have never spoken in any court before now and never promised anything. But I promise you that never again will I appear in a court of law. Of that I am determined. My resolution to turn away from crime may seem rather late but rather late than never. I am sincere and I trust you believe my words are true. Give me a chance. Just give me a hand in my desire to live an honest life and I promise you faithfully I will never let you down.'

By now in full verbal flight and clutching his notes in theatrical fashion, he seemed for all his bravery in the past a curiously vulnerable figure. He concluded his emotional plea:

'I have never used violence to any police officer but always took my medicine as it came. I know I must be punished for my crime, but I beg you to temper your justice with a little mercy. All I ask is this one chance.'

Powerful stuff, and from the heart, but despite his protestations he had made similar pleas and promises to prison governors and others before. Some kept, some not. In his emphasis on never having being shown a 'little kindness in the past' he seems to have forgotten, or chosen not to mention, the offers of help given to him to go straight by such as John Westland of the Aberdeen police and others attracted to him because of his friendly and positive attitude to a tough life.

Lord Carmont responded: 'In view of your past record I do not think I would be doing my duty if I did not consider whether it is expedient in the public interest, and for the protection of the public, that you should be detained in custody for a substantial time. But before sentencing you I must get from those who are in a position to give it to me a report on your physical and mental condition and your suitability for the sentence of preventive detention which it may be necessary to impose. I will continue the case until November 22 in the High Court in Edinburgh by which time I hope to be furnished with a report on you.'

On hearing this, Johnny made a final plea, a cry of 'just give me a chance', and he wheeled around smartly to be escorted back to the cells.

Johnny had once again played the war-hero card, but his credit was running out. Everyone who had followed his career in the papers knew full well that he had barely laid aside his Commando Green Beret in 1946 before he was back on the rooftops in a flat cap and old clothes and using his skill with explosives to steal. One Glasgow newspaper put it succinctly – 'his debt to society could not be written off by his war record on which he had already drawn heavily'.

This time, however, there was a difference. His love for Lily and his new-found taste of the honest life with her seemed genuinely to have made him regret his actions that night in Croftfoot. But it was too late. Carmont was as unbending as his public image portrayed him. When it came time to sentence Ramensky, Carmont told the man in the dock, 'I am clear from your conduct and history that you can not be trusted to abstain from crime. On the last occasion you were before this court in February 1951 you received a sentence of five years. But it is on record that but for the services rendered by you during the war a longer sentence would have been pronounced.' By now, Ramensky knew that his pleas had fallen on deaf ears.

Carmont went on: 'You have many more than the number of previous convictions required by the statute and in the course of a life of about fifty years you have received sentences of imprisonment amounting to nearly thirty years.'

All that was left was for Carmont to deliver the final blow and this time it was to be ten years. Even in the context of the 1950s, and the war against crime, this was a savage sentence. Johnny stood to attention and showed no emotion as it was announced. Lily wept, was led from the court by friends and later collapsed outside.

Clearly Johnny felt that this sentence was unfair. The facts were that he had attempted a small-scale robbery at a local garage, no one had been hurt and when he was apprehended he did not resist. Had it been a first offence then no doubt the sentence would have been a fraction of the one he received. But it was far from his first offence and Lord Carmont was clearly in no mood to play games. Johnny Ramensky had attempted to walk a straight path but had failed. Now there was no option but to pay the price.

It seems likely that Johnny's sense of injustice about the length of his sentence spurred him on to his frequent attempts to escape from Peterhead. It also marked a turning point in his life and the seeds of years of bitter resentment had been planted firmly in Johnny's psyche. If Lord Carmont had surrendered, in this one case, to an uncharacteristic softening of his stance on long sentences, would it have really turned Johnny away from crime onto the straight and narrow? No one knows. And who knows, too, what sort of sentence he would have regarded as lenient? Three years, five years, eight years? There is no easy answer, but the fact that the verdict was another huge sentence, ten years, clearly did more than send Johnny back to jail – it sentenced him to a continuing life of crime. And eventually to death behind bars.

If Johnny's remarkable trial in 1955 for the break-in at the Carmunnock Road garage showed him as a war hero down on his luck after losing his money at the Glasgow dog tracks, one of his final court appearances, more than ten years later, was a more down-to-earth affair. In 1967, there was no long-winded and fanciful plea for one last chance. There were many more years of jail time behind him. And the memory of his series of dramatic escapes from Peterhead was no longer of much interest to the public. His health was beginning to fail and he was starting to cut a slightly pathetic figure as he limped into court. And even some of the newspapers who had made money, and increased circulation figures, on the back of his exploits, were beginning to turn against him.

There was some particularly harsh comment in the *Scottish Daily Express* when he appeared in the High Court in Glasgow charged with a bank raid on his home patch of Rutherglen. Top crime reporters Ken Bryson and James Dalrymple had a go at the myth of 'Gentle Johnny' and his fame as a safecracker. It was pretty nasty stuff, with the scribes saying he was not a safe-cracker but 'a user of crude and not very predictable explosives'.

Where they got this opinion from is a mystery, as such experts in the field as the legendary Peterman have written long and often on his skill in this area. And who would believe that General 'Lucky' Laycock of the Commandos would have employed a 'user of crude and not very predictable explosives' rather than a skilled safecracker to tutor his men in time of war?

The same writers also questioned whether or not the famous rooftop 'circus' performance in Barlinnie in the 1930s ever happened! This despite the fact that, as the archives now prove, the governor and his warders were writing reports and memos on the incident. And there was the evidence of the crowds who had gathered on a hilltop outside the Barlinnie walls to watch the fun. The writers also tried to dismiss the master escapologist as 'no Houdini', claiming that his breaks from Peterhead were simply spur-of-the-moment chance-taking. It seemed that while the warders' backs were turned he simply ran off into the distance. If escaping was that easy there would be nobody in prison.

This attempted put-down of the legend also ignored the brains and planning behind escapes that had seen Johnny building dummies to hide in his cell bed to fool warders and his remarkable ability to climb walls, creep across roofs, and up and down gas and rone pipes. It was pretty sour stuff but perhaps they were toeing the editorial line of the day.

The writers were on slightly stronger ground when they attacked his non-violent image. Ramensky had played on this throughout his criminal career but it seems that he had now had a change of mind. There was, of course, the incident more than forty years earlier when Ramensky had been surprised by a householder in the middle of a robbery and assaulted her. This was a minor assault and the woman was not hurt but it was an assault nonetheless. Now the newspapers had a more serious assault to report.

The accusation in the Rutherglen trial was that Ramensky had assaulted PC Neil Wilson. The assault charge came about after his arrest and a bit of battle with the forces of the law in Main Street, Rutherglen. Even today Johnny's evidence can raise a laugh when you read it. Those in court at the time, and those following proceedings in the newspapers, must have had some real entertainment. In March 1967 Johnny, then sixty-two, appeared at Glasgow's High Court and denied breaking into the National Commercial Bank in Main Street, Rutherglen, Lanarkshire, forcing open a safe with explosives and stealing cash and foreign currency worth £252-19s-6d. In money terms this was not a great bank robbery, but it was a pretty typical Ramensky crime. The years he spent in jail seem very much at odds with the relatively small sums he stole or attempted to steal. There were no major hits on big banks in city centres – despite the fact that his Commando training and expertise would have well qualified him to carry that off.

His explanation of what happened on the night of his arrest shows a remarkable optimism on his part. Despite being caught near enough red-handed, he told a fanciful tale to the court. According to him he had been waiting for an early morning bus on the day of the raid and had walked into a backcourt adjacent to the bank in search of a toilet. He went on, without a trace of embarrassment: 'When the policeman came I was frightened and ran away. I ran down some steps, jumped over a wall and ran forty yards before I was caught. The constable hit me with his baton as I ran. Just then my arms flew out and accidentally hit him in the face. There was a scuffle and we both fell to the ground. The policeman jumped on my chest with his knees. I had nothing to do with the explosion in the bank. I was just going home after spending the night in my sister's house nearby.'

All a bit of a sob story: the old lag pursued by the cops when trying to lead a peaceful life. Aye, right, as they say in these parts. And the evidence showed otherwise. In the jacket he was wearing when caught there was a handle for a drill which had been found in the bank. Detectives also found a small piece of wire identical to that found wrapped around the handle of the night safe. There was also the small matter of a quantity of gelignite he was carrying, in this case Polar Ammon, a type of explosive much favoured by the safe-blowing fraternity.

Despite his reputation as a man who used as little explosive as necessary, enough Polar Ammon was deployed that night to shatter the peace and quiet of douce Main Street, Rutherglen after dark, and the 'wee red lums' got a good rattling. The bang that attracted the attention of the police was powerful enough to shatter a few windows and wake the residents sleeping peacefully near the bank.

Clearly this was a massive explosion and was far greater than would be expected for a job of this size. A highly experienced safecracker told me that if you get the right quantity of 'gelly' into a lock and round the edges of a safe you can put your shoulder to the safe door when firing the charge in order to maximise the effect of the explosive in moving the door. Mind you, he also said that it was not a method he used himself! Incidentally the same old villain, who knew Johnny well, told me that he thinks he picked up some of his expertise in the Peterhead prison quarry as well as in mines.

Johnny was an expert in 'gelly' with a detailed knowledge of the effects of different kinds of explosive. Polar Ammon, as used in Rutherglen, produces a circular explosion, while Polar Unigel tends to strike down and Polar Ajax blows outward. The safe-cracking expert clearly thought it was highly unusual that so much explosive was used in the Rutherglen job and that it was not Johnny's style. He was losing his touch.

For the trial, Johnny had the services of Nicholas Fairbairn who went on to be a flamboyant and controversial QC and politician, and Joe Beltrami, that remarkable lawyer known as 'The Great Defender' or 'The Sage of West Nile Street'.

When called to Barlinnie and in their pre-trial conferences, both Joe Beltrami, who defended Johnny many times, and Nicky Fairbairn took a bit of a shine to their client. They found him, as most people did, an attractive personality and were determined to get him off the assault charge. They, of all people, knew that the sort of gear Johnny had in his possession on arrest was not quite consistent with a man spending a quiet night at his sister's and that any denial was probably doomed. Johnny had some further bad luck on this job – the safe he blew was empty and the few hundreds he had stolen came from a drawer in the back of the bank. It was small beer indeed, but he had neglected to open another nearby drawer which did contain thousands in neat bundles of used fivers and tenners, which would have made for a dream haul.

When he called his legal team to Barlinnie, where he was being held to await the trial, Johnny seemed to be prepared to face facts on the safe blowing, but the assault charge was another story. Johnny was by now well steeped in the details of his own legend as recorded by the newspapers. He was a proud man who both enjoyed and nurtured his fame as 'Gentle Johnny'. No pipsqueak cop, not long out of police college, should be allowed to tarnish that. All he had done, after all, was defend himself.

In the prison Johnny made it abundantly clear to his lawyers that this accusation, false to his mind, was more important than the details – or indeed the punishment coming his way for a run-of-the-mill bank robbery. The real job of Fairbairn and Beltrami was to deal with the assault charge and Nicky cross-examined Constable Wilson for half an hour on how he had chased and caught Johnny.

Neil Wilson told the court: 'I am afraid I had to use my baton. I saw him climb down a rone pipe from the bank roof and gave chase. Ramensky ran down some steeps, climbed over a six foot wall and ran off. When I caught him I gripped him by the shoulders and pulled him round. We had only gone back one or two yards when he lashed out and started fighting me. He swung out with his fist and hit me on the face. It felt very sore. We fell to the ground then Constable Clowes arrived and joined in the fight.'

The Advocate Depute, Mr R. King-Murray, asked how he had managed to subdue Ramensky. The policeman replied: 'I drew my baton and aimed at his shoulder, which is recognised police procedure, but his head came in contact with my baton. This ended the struggle and I handcuffed his hands together before taking him to Rutherglen police office. I did not know at the time the accused was Johnny Ramensky.'

Constable Clowes then added what could be construed as a compliment to Johnny as a fighting man: 'We did not know what age he was at the time. He struggled like a man of twenty-one.'

The assault charge was dealt with by way of a 'not proven' verdict so on that, at least, Johnny got a result. But the judge, Lord Thomson, told the accused: 'You have been found guilty of a very serious offence – the crime of breaking into a bank, opening lockfast places, stealing money and blowing open a safe. I can sentence you to no less than four years' imprisonment.' This was roughly a week in jail for every pound stolen!

Johnny nodded acknowledgement to a small group of friends in court and took the familiar steps back to the cells. Lily, who by now was used to seeing her husband being sentenced and led away from her, was remarkably philosophical when the press called at her home in Eglinton Street. She said: 'Before his arrest I had fourteen months with Johnny but now I look on him as going back to his second home. I will be here when he comes out. But I could not honestly say that Johnny will never go away from me again. He is a craftsman who just refused to retire from his trade.' Wise words. Sad words.

Johnny's contrasting behaviour at these two trials is intriguing and gives an insight into his mind both at this time and during his career in crime from the age of eleven. Dr Kathy Charles, a forensic psychologist who lectures at Edinburgh Napier University, is a recognised expert in the field. Her perceptive comments and analysis are revealing. Kathy commented:

'Johnny Ramensky was by no means a typical criminal. It

was not just the nature of his offending which set him apart from other offenders but also his abilities and personality. It is fashionable these days to label a prolific criminal like Johnny as a psychopath because the word conjures up all kinds of dramatic images in the public's mind. Fictional and factual psychopaths generate an extra frisson when discussed, as though they are set apart from the average criminal. In addition there is a large body of scientific psychological research demonstrating that psychopaths are physiologically different in many ways to the normal population. It would be too simplistic to label Johnny as a psychopath, though. It is true that he has some characteristics which are commonly found in psychopaths, but he also has many which are in direct conflict with such a diagnosis.'

Johnny's criminal career and his related courtroom activities can be more usefully considered as a manifestation of his sensation-seeking and an adaptation to his environment. Kathy went on to say: 'Johnny's early life was harsh and by his own admission he associated with "urchins" from an early age. Even now, a century later, being born and raised in a socially deprived area is a significant risk factor for childhood and adult offending. Added to this is Johnny's loss of his father aged just seven. It is not known if he had any other kind of father figure in his life, but an absence of an adult male role model can leave some children vulnerable to seeking acceptance and approval from peers rather than adults. It is clear that Johnny ended up taking prolific offenders as his role models. This, combined with Johnny's "urchin" peers, is very likely to have led him to crime, as he claims in his 1955 trial.

'In many ways his early life and his early criminal record (age eleven) are similar to what we routinely read in the newspapers about today's young offenders or "Neds". The historical context of Johnny does introduce other variables for consideration though. Johnny's knowledge and ability with explosives was acquired in the early part of his life when he worked in coalmines. This is something which youngsters are no longer exposed to. The opportunity for him to use his talents in the war also allowed his criminal behaviour to be expressed in a legitimate and beneficial way for a period of time – again, something which is unlikely to be afforded to anyone these days. This episode of legitimately using explosives arguably shaped some of Johnny's later courtroom behaviour and strategy.'

Kathy commented on the fact that Johnny lived to be sixty-seven, which she felt is a good age given the time period in which he lived and his lifestyle. She pointed out he spent more than forty of those years in prison with a period of time in the Commandos, meaning that the majority of his life was heavily structured and institutionalised. Although he frequently absconded from prison he appeared unable (or unwilling) to sufficiently modify his behaviour to prevent repeated incarceration. His escapes were surprisingly short-lived and occasionally done on impulse. 'This pattern of activity is observed in psychopathic individuals and it not only reflects a failure to learn, but also an indifference to prison and other forms of punishment. In Johnny's case it seems that the escape in itself was the goal, rather than prolonged liberty.

'Despite his start in life and his adult behaviour, Johnny appears to lack a cardinal feature of the psychopathic offender: the callous, unemotional trait. Johnny's reputation for being non-violent and for not targeting domestic properties suggest that he had compassion and did not want to target vulnerable people. It is far easier to burgle domestic properties than commercial ones and given that Johnny's bank robberies often yielded modest returns, he could have undoubtedly made more money with high-frequency domestic burglaries. Offenders today who operate alone and seek a steady income from crime tend to commit high-volume domestic break-ins rather than risk a large commercial operation. It is this aspect of Johnny's character which makes it difficult to classify him as a psychopathic offender.'

According to Kathy, Johnny was undoubtedly a sensation-seeker and many of his actions seem to have been motivated by a desire to escape a state of under-arousal or lack of stimulation, rather than out of callousness. She said: 'The sensation-seeking trait can take many forms and is essentially about seeking varied, novel and complex sensations and experiences. Sometimes sensation-seekers will engage in extreme sports, be promiscuous, cause fights or take a lot of drugs. In other cases an individual may be more internally driven and be preoccupied with dreaming and fantasy. Whatever form sensation-seeking takes, there are underlying biological mechanisms which drive the individual towards stimulation. Johnny reveals his sensation-seeking through his offending, his prison escapes, his military career, his gambling and his involvement in intellectual jousting when in prison. All of these activities would cause significant physiological and psychological arousal, which would be experienced as fear in many other people. It is also noteworthy that Johnny appears to be particularly hardy and can withstand poor conditions in prison, terrible weather when he escapes from prison and even illness and accident. This ability points to a reduced capacity to feel pain – another characteristic of sensation-seekers – and is also incredibly useful in Johnny's line of work.

'A desire to represent oneself in court also fits with a sensation-seeker who likes attention. It is an unusual strategy and is sometimes seen in offenders or alleged offenders who are either very narcissistic or who are psychopathic. In most individuals the idea of defending yourself stems from a belief that, despite no formal legal training, the individual knows better than the man or woman who has spent many years studying and practising law. It suggests a very egocentric perspective along with a disregard for the abilities of others. It can be an effective strategy with jurors if the defendant is sufficiently charming or appeals to their background, but it is not a "get out of jail free" card and is generally seen as a risky strategy.'

After years of being the jailhouse lawyer and engaging in lengthy correspondence with various authorities, Johnny must have believed he would be a dab hand at defending himself. After this approach failed him in 1955 he seemed to abandon it in favour of a QC. If nothing else, Johnny had realised that it was probably the end of the line for his charm offensive and war-hero approach in front of legal personnel.

Kathy added: 'It is certainly interesting to note the change in Johnny's behaviour between his 1955 and 1967 court appearances. In 1955 we see a man who has resisted many efforts by friends and professionals to help him go straight and desist from crime. Although repentant in his speech, he still has a spark about him and a little defiance. Johnny is enjoying being the showman and believes in himself. He hopes his war record and difficult childhood will act as mitigation (as they have done before) but this suggests an inability to see his behaviour as others see it and to recognise the climate of "crime crackdown" in Glasgow at that time. This could be deemed characteristic of the psychopath – a form of narcissistic thinking which prevents the individual from seeing himself as anything other than justified, but in Johnny's case it fits more comfortably with his belief that crime is one big game and that he'll give anything a try.

'The events leading up to the offence in 1955 are indicative of a failure to consider consequences. Johnny acted whilst feeling angry after losing his money gambling. He was careless in the burglary because for a short time the pursuit of lost money was more important to him than his liberty or, indeed, his lovely Lily Mulholland. Johnny's speech is also peppered with comments which express his bitterness at the legal system, even though he now depends on its mercy: "I have already served three life sentences for my misdeeds in the past. The law has had more than its pound of flesh" suggests that his time served should do more than pay his debt to society, but should also be a kind of equity for future offending. He feels he should be treated differently from other offenders. An unrealistic approach, but one which he cannot help but mention as he feels his behaviour is justified in some way.

'He also tries to shift the focus from himself to his wife in an effort to make any punishment seem as though it would be punishing her rather than him. These strategies ultimately fail him on this occasion but show that he is capable of a degree of emotional manipulation. Up until he is sentenced to ten more years Johnny certainly has some spirit left in him and his speech reflects a man who is trying a variety of approaches with the confidence that one of them will work.'

In Kathy's view the 1967 trial was quite different. This time Gentle Johnny, who had previously been unceremoniously hit on the head by a policeman without provocation, was now accused of brawling on the floor and struggling 'like a man of twenty-one' against two policemen. He was also accused of breaking into a bank and stealing more than £250. Kathy said: 'Instead of admitting his deeds and producing another heartfelt plea for mitigation, Johnny disputed what happened and presented what sounded like a fanciful version of events. He no longer associated himself proudly with his safecracking skills and instead claims to have been looking for a toilet near the bank. Of his assault charges he claims that his arms "flew out" and that he "accidentally" hit the officer in the face. This is weak by any standard. It should be noted that the officer's account of fighting with Johnny is equally unbelievable when he says that he aimed at Johnny's shoulder with his baton but that Johnny's head somehow got in the way. Neither party seems willing to say that there was a bit of a dirty fight.'

Between 1955 and 1967 Johnny underwent a change in his attitude and strategy. As Kathy Charles pointed out: 'At the age of fifty he was still using the script that he'd apparently used for much of his life. He did not deny his crimes, he traded on his war record and his tough upbringing and he had a good deal of confidence in his efforts to secure leniency. Johnny had always believed that crime was a game. He was under no illusions that what he was doing was wrong and he knew it was a "fair cop" when he was caught. Johnny had respect for police officers and prison staff who he clearly saw as a kind of "friends and family" within the crime game. The stringent sentence he received in 1955 seems to have affected him and his confidence, though.

'The man that appeared in the dock twelve years later appeared to have become desperate in some respects. He had fought with policemen and chosen to make up bizarre accounts of what happened, which was totally out of character for a man who had always showed incredible integrity (considering his occupation). Johnny now lacked the confidence to try and present a favourable impression of himself and instead chose to deny responsibility. There is a distinct loss of vitality in the now aging safecracker. Although this looks as though he is going out with a whimper rather than a bang, it does show some insight on his part and an acknowledgement of how others must have come to view him. Perhaps he had come to realise that denying involvement is a better bet than trying to justify involvement.'

Johnny was quite remarkable when considered alongside his peers. Although his early life unfolded in a sadly familiar way for a prolific offender, what followed was a striking departure from what anyone working with offenders today would recognise. Johnny's literacy was exceptional – many prisoners (even today) cannot read or write beyond a very basic level. The compassion he showed for his fellow prisoners and his desire to improve their conditions is also a credit to him. Kathy Charles observed: 'Johnny could not be called selfish in that respect and did not limit his letter-writing to self-interest. That his letter-writing also extended to get well messages to senior police officers and messages from the front to prison governors just adds to his complexity. Also of note is the manner in which Johnny conducted himself both in and out of prison – his fastidiousness and the way he shunned violence make him exceptional and certainly makes it very difficult to try and place the psychopath label on him. Johnny does not fit into the typical prolific offender pigeonhole. He was not an intimidating hard man who built a reputation on brutality. Johnny seems to have truly lived up to his "Gentle Johnny" sobriquet.'

Kathy is of the opinion that Johnny most likely persisted with his criminal enterprises because it was all he knew. Prison and crime would have seemed more normal to him than law-abiding family life. It can be difficult to understand why someone would repeatedly shun the opportunity for liberty and support, but that is because most people fear the loss of their liberty and home comforts. Comfort and security come from what you know and are familiar with. Johnny knew crime, explosives and prison and that is what he repeatedly returned to. Kathy concluded that: 'A life on the outside would never have satisfied Johnny's desire for stimulation. His high-stakes gambling is about as close as he could get on the outside to the thrills he needed. As the years passed Johnny developed a sound insight into his own psychology and he expressed this in a letter to a journalist: "I am a crook, always have been and there is no turning back." As others have done before, one cannot help but wonder what Johnny could have achieved if he'd been able to satisfy his personality through non-criminal means.'

This persistent refusal to give up the buzz of what Johnny called 'the game' is desperately sad. He was trading brief moments of so-called excitement, and the adrenalin rush that accompanied them, for long, long periods of deprivation in prison.

# 14

# THE CURIOUS CARFIN
# INCIDENT IN THE NIGHT

Long stretches in jail in the company of men in a similar situation – looking ahead to years of confinement before you can even dream of release and a return to society – can create friendships that last for life. For Johnny one of the consolations of the years behind bars in the 1960s was that he became close to that other remarkable Lanarkshire villain, Willie 'Sonny' Leitch, previously mentioned as the legendary escaper known as the 'Saughton Harrier'.

Their paths had crossed over the years in various jails including Craiginches, Saughton and Peterhead but their friendship really grew in Barlinnie and Perth. The real start of their relationship came with a meeting in Barlinnie that Willie remembers well. Willie, though younger, had a somewhat similar Lanarkshire background to the young Yonus Ramanauckas. He, too, was a teenage lawbreaker, though he found his action in his native Lanarkshire rather than the infamous Gorbals. Willie's family were respectable folk, but he, like Johnny, found walking 'the crooked path' provided him with the excitement he needed. Despite family opposition he went down the mines, again like Johnny.

In a strange twist of fate, Willie first heard of Ramensky as a youngster, when Johnny's activities led to Willie's dad appearing in court as a witness. This was at a trial for theft involving a stolen miner's lamp. On a 'social' visit back to the Craigneuk area, Johnny took the opportunity to acquire some equipment helpful to his 'night job' as a cat burglar. He broke into the sheds of the colliery and stole a battery of the type used to power miners' lamps. This was ideal for use with detonators. When the break-in was discovered it was found that the battery had belonged to Willie's father, who was called on as a witness in the subsequent trial. The court appearance was the first time Willie was to see Johnny Ramensky, even by then a legend in Lanarkshire. Willie said: 'My dad told me about the court visit to identify his lamp and I said to myself, "Whoever stole my dad's lamp, I'll get him when I grow up."'

In the meantime Willie had joined the Navy and had found himself in all sort of scrapes and a few foreign jails in his time, escaping briefly from one of the toughest in Singapore. Like Johnny, Willie was street-sharp and he was earmarked for promotion in the Navy, had he been able to keep out of the brig. Again like Johnny, in civvy street, jail was almost a regular home from home. An incident involving a car found him in the Bar-L – though according to Willie, one of his mates nicked it and left him to take the blame. In Barlinnie, Willie was to meet the man whose name he still remembered from his schooldays. Johnny was down from Peterhead for visits and sitting at a table with some of the most infamous names in Glasgow gangland – among them Tank McGuinness, Bobby Campbell (father of T. C., one of the men wrongly convicted for the Ice Cream Wars murders), James Kemp (Evil Jim) and Andy Lawson.

The talk turned to Shepton Mallet, the English jail that was one of the hardest in all of Britain. Someone mentioned Willie had had a spell there and the call came: 'Hey, come ower here.' Willie promptly joined the hard men for, as he said: 'Well, you didnae say no to that mob.' Johnny asked, had he really been in the Mallet? Willie had a strong feeling he was not far away from a fight, but he didn't scare easily. Johnny then asked: 'Know who I am?' and Willie replied, 'Aye, I'm going to break your fucking face – you're the man who stole my dad's pit lamp from Shields colliery.'

Neither Willie's threat – one of his nicknames was 'Danger Man' – nor the story of what had happened at Shields was anything other than accurate. The hard men who had called Willie over to join them at the table admired his guts in standing up to them, and the humour inherent in the situation, and it ended with everyone killing themselves laughing. That, as they say, is prison life.

But Shepton Mallet has a more macabre connection to the Ramensky story, as Willie told Johnny in a later Bar-L conversation. After the Navy and his service in Korea, Willie was sent to the Mallet for some offence or other. This was a place where military executions were carried out and Edmund Dunn, who had killed a taxi driver in Germany, was due to hang. The executions at the Mallet were unusual as they were carried out Australian-style – rather than the executioner slipping a bolt and the condemned man falling into a pit, the victim was attached to the rope and pulled into the air and strangled that way.

These macabre happenings took place in a part of the building which had once been a sort of baronial-style assembly hall. It was, at this point in time, a bit of a mess and Willie was despatched from his cell – with others, some of them Scots – to tidy the place up. It wasn't really necessary or urgent as in the end Edmund Dunn got a reprieve, but in the tidying-up process Willie came across racks filled with parcels of tarred paper bundles. There were also heavy ammunition boxes that 'weighed a ton' and were difficult to move and tidy up. As a good Scottish hard man would do, Willie tore some of the paper parcels open to see what was inside. He knew nothing of the Commandos' exploits in Rome and got the shock of his life at what he saw – paintings of Eva Braun, Hitler, Goering and Hess and paperwork referring to much of the Nazi high command. Years later, in Barlinnie, Willie Leitch told Johnny of his bizarre find. Ex-Commando John Ramsay must have had a laugh as he told Willie 'so that's where they took it', meaning the plunder nabbed by the advancing Allies.

Johnny told his fellow convicts that he had seen the paintings, not in the Mallet, but in houses he had been ordered to break into in Germany and Italy during the war. This shared interest led to Willie Leitch forming a strong friendship with Johnny – a friendship that was to last till the day of Johnny's death.

The 'ammunition' boxes were another story. What was inside the heavy boxes, which had large numbers stencilled on the outside, is a mystery. Is it too much of a leap of imagination to suggest it might well have been some of the art objects and jewellery taken from the safes when Rome fell to the Allies? Gold is said to have disappeared from Rome, so who knows? It is one of many unsolved mysteries that still surround Johnny Ramensky's extraordinary life.

But perhaps there is a partial explanation. Some time after the war there was an unusual burglary in Lanarkshire. Daft as it may seem, for a place so far from the sea, there was a naval storage depot in Carfin, a village much famed for its grotto and known as the Scottish Lourdes. It was not far from the stamping ground of Johnny's youth in Glenboig and Craigneuk. Willie Leitch knew all about this break-in and tells a strange story. Apparently, around the depot, you could see deliveries being made and all sorts of interesting stuff was being unloaded. Lorry loads of tinned cake and egg powder were seen being deposited into the sheds. Tempting stuff in the post-war days when there was still a black market. A villain Willie knew from his Saughton days was tipped off and decided to 'tan' the depot with his pals to get their hands on cake and other black market goodies. But inside the darkened sheds their torches showed, according to Willie, something a lot more interesting than powdered egg. The light shone on jewelled statuary and glistening precious stones. And in the shed were 'ammunition' boxes and the numbers on them were said to be the same or similar to those Willie had seen in Shepton Mallet.

The story goes that the burglars thought they had won the pools but needed transport to get the stuff out. They disappeared back over the fence for a lorry to cart the loot away. On their return to the depot they were nabbed as security people had discovered a breach in the fence. The thieves told the arresting party that they had been tipped off about the haul by 'The Pope' – a particularly Lanarkshire joke since all this was supposed to have happened in Carfin with all its Catholic connections. It is still rumoured in those parts that the statues and other valuable objects had been taken from Rome near the end of war, as the British advanced and the Germans retreated, in order to prevent them being looted and taken to Germany. According to the rumours, when things settled down after the war this stuff was returned to Italy. Fantasy? Who knows? But Willie Leitch says that Johnny told him some of the numbers on the ammo boxes in Carfin, which he had told him about, sounded familiar. . . .

# 15

# CIVVY STREET

Johnny Ramensky spent most of his life in jail, paying the price for his crimes. But when he was a free man, between sentences, he seemed to enjoy the good life. He had family, friends and admirers, and a life which many would have envied. After his release from jail, Johnny always seemed to have the best of intentions – a desire to go straight, to live a normal life doing normal things – but it didn't usually take too long for the old demons to raise their heads. Soon he would tire of normality and be on the lookout for a new thrill, new dangers. If it was the high life he needed, the thrill of the big gamble, then he'd be looking for easy money from crime to fund it. But before that, he usually managed to enjoy at least a bit of normal life before his thoughts turned once again to cracking safes.

In the early 1960s Johnny had a couple of fairly long spells of domestic bliss at home with Lily and her family from her previous marriage. During these spells he successfully resisted the dangerous excitement of a return to the criminal life, at least for a few months. One of Glasgow's best-known reporters, Ron Belbin, met him on his release from Barlinnie in June 1963. It was not a new experience for Ron as he had also interviewed Johnny in December 1954 on the occasion of a previous release. He found Johnny's attitude apparently changed from their meeting eleven years earlier. Johnny had a hugely unwarranted optimism that all would go well in the future and that it would be different this time. Johnny began the interview by harking back to 1954:

'Then life on the outside beat me. I had served two long sentences for safe blowing after the war. Despite even my marriage to Lily early in 1955 I could not settle down. After the years of prison routine normal life was too difficult.

'There is none of that strangeness this time. I have been on a training for freedom scheme for months past, clocking out of Saughton Prison in the early morning to work on housing schemes in Edinburgh and returning to my cell, just like any other man going home, each evening. I had a weekend visit to Glasgow every six weeks and also managed to see Lily regularly between these trips. It was nine months of almost complete freedom which proved to be a wonderful system of rehabilitation – even if the money for the work I was doing was not too good! The important thing is I have no qualms about life outside this time.'

How sad that this confident assertion and his praise for the training for freedom programme was to prove so falsely optimistic in his case. But then, he always was something special and a bit different. Johnny did not fit any mould – even one carefully designed to help prisoners return to normal life after a long sentence.

It would not be all that many months after this confident interview before the safecracker was again in court and again behind bars. But before that there would be a spell of happiness with Lily and some time to enjoy his celebrity. And enjoy it he did. In conversation he was never boastful about his exploits during the war though he did not hide them from anyone who asked about them. But he always kept a few secrets for the diary he dreamed of writing and there is no doubt that his record as Scotland's leading jailbreaker provided him with some quiet satisfaction.

Thanks to his newspaper notoriety, his face was one of the best known in the country. His noted celebrity in the north-east by now extended to the whole country and he had always been a 'player' in the Glasgow crime scene. He could not take a couple of steps on the street without being recognised. At times it could be irritating, but like a stage or TV star he enjoyed being recognised – indeed on occasion being pestered – more than he enjoyed being ignored. Except, of course, if he was on 'active service' as a cat burglar. Then he was careful not to be noticed by any man in a uniform with black and white checks on his cap.

The nature of his celebrity is demonstrated by a holiday experience in Ayr. He decided that he and Lily Mulholland should have an away break together. After all, she had waited patiently for years for him and, heaven knows, she did not have many such moments. Lily, who stood by him with great loyalty, deserved what would now be called 'quality time'.

The couple decided to head down the old A77 dual carriage-way to Ayr, where their appearance caused a mini-sensation. Everywhere in the seaside town, not many miles from Glasgow, they were spotted by locals and holidaymakers alike. In summertime in the 1960s, it seemed at times that half of Glasgow went 'doon the watter' to numerous holiday resorts on the Firth of Clyde for a break from the grind of factory, steelworks, shipyard or mine. And the holidaymakers all knew of Johnny Ramensky. It was almost what you could call Ramenskymania and it peaked when Johnny took Lily into a little café in Ayr for a snack. A crowd of more than 100 gathered outside the place to peek through the windows for a glimpse of the infamous criminal and war hero. In the end the police had to be called to tell the crowds to 'move along now' and let Johnny and Lily get on with their holiday. It prompted Johnny to remark: 'It is the first time I have ever had the police helping me to escape from anything.'

That night reporter Ron Belbin also accompanied Johnny and Lily to the summer show in the famous old Gaiety, the theatre owned and managed by Leslie and Eric Popplewell. A night at the Gaiety was a must for anyone on holiday down the Clyde coast. The couple were given a personal welcome by Eric that night, according to the star of the show, comedian Johnny Beattie. Eric had even shown them to their stall seats. He loved to have celebrities in the house and made a fuss of them whenever he could. And after the commotion of the arrival of Johnny and Lily at the theatre and their progress to the stalls, watched with excitement by a full house in holiday good humour, Eric asked Johnny Beattie if it would be all right to bring them backstage to his dressing room for a nice little drink at the interval.

It was more than all right. The star was delighted to get the chance to meet a man who for years had filled the news pages of the Glasgow papers. He remembers the night well. He found Johnny and Lily a friendly, 'ordinary wee Glasgow couple', delightful to meet. And even now, all these years later, he still can't get over how unimposing Johnny was and says it was almost impossible to imagine the mild-looking man sitting in his dressing room, sharing a modest tincture or two with him, as the man behind the lurid headlines. Legendary escaper, Commando and safecracker as he was, Johnny did not at all look the part. He smiled and he talked, enjoying the company of the famous actor and comedian and everyone was having a pleasant evening of laughter and fun in the old seaside theatre. The comedian did not introduce prisons or war service to the conversation and neither did Johnny. His host that night says there was not an inch of boastfulness or vanity in Gentle Johnny and the chat in the star's dressing room was of every-day things – Ayr's beach, the weather, the cafés, and the throngs of holidaymakers.

Ron Belbin went back to the couple's hotel with them when the show was over and the reporter noted, as Johnny sat there remarking that the day's experience had been 'overwhelming', that he was tanned and extremely smartly dressed. The reporter echoed the remarks of the comedian: 'He looked the last person anyone would have thought of as a newly released convict and a man who had spent more than thirty years behind bars.'

Not looking like a criminal is a natural advantage for someone bent on a criminal life. However, Johnny was still talking about going straight. 'I have never been healthier in my life and I am eager and ready to start work. I have had the offer of a job in Glasgow and hope to start as soon as this brief holiday is over.' Dream on . . .

The night at the Gaiety was an unusual excursion into the world of showbiz but for years folk music played a role in adding to Johnny's fame and appeal to the public. All the newspaper attention and the stories that showed him as an out of the ordinary criminal attracted the attention of folk song writers, singers and audiences. He is particularly remembered in two remarkable songs written about him. 'Ramensky Must Go Free' was written by the actor Roddy McMillan, famous for his portrayal of Para Handy on television and a succession of acclaimed roles in the Scottish theatre. 'The Ballad of Johnny Ramensky', which uses the tune of an old song, 'Jamie Foyers', was published in 1959 by the late Glasgow MP and Labour Party veteran Norman Buchan, who was an avid folk song collector. At the time the MP was quoted as saying: 'It is undoubtedly true that almost all people, regardless of the rights and wrongs of his case, felt some sympathy for the man who detested prison to strongly that he broke out of Scotland's strongest jail five times.'

Buchan was, for a time, a teacher in Johnny's old patch of Rutherglen, and his song was sung on television by guitarist Enoch Kent of the folksong foursome The Reivers. But the group did not feature the song when doing a gig for the prisoners in Barlinnie in 1959. It probably seemed inappropriate at the time, but maybe it could have gained the fame of Johnny Cash's 'Folsom Prison Blues' if they had included it. The cons would have loved it. Hamish Imlach also featured the ballad in his act. A snatch of it went like this:

He's been in prison for the maist of his days
And 'I must hae freedom' is a' that he says
There are nae horizons in a twenty-foot cell
And bitter the music o' a harsh prison bell.

'Ramensky Must Go Free' featured in the early life experience of
Tam Purvey, who spent some time in his youth in an approved
school in Bishopbriggs near Glasgow. He recounts how Johnny
and the song changed his attitude, and his life, for the good. Tam
says the school set him on the right track after a dodgy start as a
youngster. He was one of around 120 boys aged from fourteen
to sixteen in the institution. It was pretty tough 'with plenty of
violence' and a fierce pecking order among the boys who 'wore
baggy jeans and a blue sort of Royal Navy shirt. We had black
working shoes, and a haircut to make sure you would be easily
recognised if you absconded.'

Tam says: 'I was a member of our folk-singing class and there
would be about twenty boys in the class under Mr Hughes
(a.k.a. "Cannonball") who played guitar and was a great influence on us. I have him to thank for any success in my life.

'In the folk class we all sang "Let Ramensky Go", with real
gusto. We were also told of Johnny's wartime exploits, and I
remember being very impressed and never forgot the story. I
think Mr Hughes knew that the Ramensky song and his life
story would fire the boys' imagination and it did. He was a
clever man, Mr Hughes.'

So, long after his patriotic and brave exploits, the legend of
Johnny Ramensky played a powerful role in sorting out young
lives. No doubt he would have been very proud of that.

Johnny could undoubtedly be affable to the man in the street
and he could acquire friends in the police and the prison service,
but he was not always so upfront as he was with Ron Belbin
when dealing with the press. Perhaps some *News of the World*
money may have eased that particular friendship. Another
Glasgow newspaper legend, John Quinn, has a slightly different

tale to tell. Johnny could be wary of the press, and the matchbox story is a case in point.

John Quinn had a long career in Glasgow's newspapers as a reporter who rose to the heights of news editor and was, additionally, for many years, the top boxing writer in the country. He is also the man credited with attaching the nickname 'Bible John' to Scotland's most infamous serial killer in 1968 and 1969. The Bible John saga was a highlight in John's career, but even early on, as a humble foot soldier for the press, he was involved in crime reporting. In newspapers in Glasgow such work was, and is, a major part of the job.

On this occasion, a young John Quinn was told by his boss about a tip-off that Johnny Ramensky was abroad in the city. John was despatched to get an interview and he found himself outside the front door of the famous man one morning. He rang the bell time after time, but got no response. Feeling a bit desperate and not at all anxious to return to the office empty-handed, he noticed an old matchbox lying on the landing of the close. He picked it up, took a sheet from his notebook and penned a little note to the master criminal. He pointed out that he was new on the job and that he really needed to get a story. John explained it was vital to his career as a reporter. A few words – anything – would be a great help. He had to have an interview.

He poured it on pretty thick. When he finished, he popped the note into the matchbox and thrust it through the letterbox and waited. Sure enough, after some time, the matchbox was pushed back out the letterbox. 'This is it, I've made it, I've got a story,' thought the ambitious young reporter. Wrong. The note was still inside and when John took it out and turned it over the reverse side had on it a scrawled message from Johnny. It said simply: 'Too bad'.

Maybe if it had been a brown envelope stuffed with readies the answer might have been different. Or maybe it was just that the great escaper knew very well when it was time to talk, when it was time to be that legendary likeable rogue, and when it was time to keep quiet.

That Johnny and Lily were happy together, at least in the early years, was pretty obvious to anyone who knew them. Freddy Sutherland was a publican at Anderston Cross in the city centre in the mid-1960s and remembers a small dapper gentleman coming into the pub on occasions. Freddy does not remember his Christian name, but his surname was Clark. This was Tom Clark, who was Johnny's 'special chum' in Barlinnie in the late 1920s and early 1930s and at different times his bookie's clerk and safe-blasting assistant. On occasions Johnny accompanied this gent. Freddy says Johnny wore the standard garb of the man about town of the times – jacket, collar and tie, the ubiquitous Crombie overcoat and soft hat. No jeans, trainers and sweat-shirts in those days. Johnny and Tom Clark enjoyed many a pleasant hour in Freddy's pub and Lily often came along with them. She used the name Ramsay and in this company, in the pub, Johnny was happy to be known as John Ramsay.

Freddy Sutherland remembers that on their weekly visits to the pub the wee group was always well dressed, well mannered and although they drank very little there was a lot of laughter as tales were told and in general there was an 'effervescent' atmo-sphere in the pub when they were around. The retired publican remembers that Johnny and Lily came across as real pals as well as husband and wife, one of the nicest things you can say of a married couple.

But he also remembers an occasion in the pub when a minor crack appeared in Johnny's reputation for taking things calmly. But its re-telling does little to dent his Gentle John image, rather it underlines the caring Ramensky temperament. Apparently Tom Clark had hidden some explosives in his coal bunker, but he had not let his wife into the secret. Unknowingly, Mrs Clark had shovelled the explosives, mixed with the coal, onto the fire. The explosion injured the Clark children who were playing in front of the fire at the time. The story has it that such carelessness with explosives drove Johnny crazy and he gave his pal a bit of a verbal doing as a reminder to be more careful with 'gelly' and such like when looking for secret hiding places. If anyone had respect for explosives and knew how to handle them it was John Ramensky.

Interestingly Johnny's niece, Dorothy McNab, remembers hearing of the incident as a child in her home in Rutherglen. Johnny was certainly not best pleased with his chum 'Wee Tommy', as Dorothy called him, on that occasion.

Freddy Sutherland makes an interesting observation about Johnny's acrobatics on darkened roofs when out on the prowl and his exploits in breaking out of jails: 'I have never seen a pair of hands and wrists like Johnny Ramensky's. His wrists were thicker than my fists.' The publican colourfully described Johnny as, 'around five foot seven and looking like a cross between James Cagney and Pope John Paul II'. Clearly that physical prowess was a significant asset during throughout his criminal career.

# 16

## AMONG FRIENDS

In the early 1960s, during that idyllic spell of freedom between the Croftfoot garage job and the failed Rutherglen bank robbery, Johnny spent some time in the huge Glasgow Southside scheme of Castlemilk which, as part of the post-war drive to provide good housing for working folk, became home to the astonishing figure of around 60,000 people decanted from the city slums. This was similar to the population of Perth at the time and the snag was that the well-meaning authorities, in their rush to provide inside toilets and kitchens with Formica tables, forgot to factor pubs, libraries, swimming pools and cinemas into the equation. No wonder the place became something of hotbed for crime in its early years. The badly needed amenities were added many years down the line, and the huge scheme began to change in character. For the better.

For a spell in the 1960s Johnny became a well-known figure in what the early denizens of the place referred to as 'the Mulk'. One of his pals in this part of his life was Tony Russell, a remarkable ex-miner and soldier who served with both the Argyll and Sutherland Highlanders and the Gordon Highlanders. Tony was of Lithuanian descent and left Scotland many years ago to start a new life in the then prosperous coal mines of Alberta, Canada, which produced high-quality, high-heat-generating coal too good for domestic use, but ideal for exporting to Japan where post-war factories were manufacturing at full blast. With the sort of remark that proves the old adage that you can take the man out of Glasgow, but not Glasgow out of the man, Tony told me that this black gold looked like 'what we would call the dross at the bottom of the bunker.' Tony, now nearing ninety, with his memory and mind working almost as well as ever, lives in the beautiful Rocky Mountains town of Canmore, where the deep mines are now closed, just like their counterparts in Lanarkshire.

Before he met Johnny, Tony had heard much about him from his father, Joe Gazausis, who had come from eastern Europe to Scotland along with the Ramanauckas family and those thousands of other immigrants at the turn of the twentieth century. Old Joe, who had crossed the North Sea to come to the mines, never fully mastered English and in the habit of the times eventually anglicised his name. He had vivid memories of working underground in Lanarkshire in the Glenboig clay mine and indeed he liked to tell Tony that he was the man who honed Johnny's shot-firing skills when they were underground together. It is clear he must have been a really first-class mentor to Johnny and the young Ramensky was clearly a quick learner.

Tony's family lived in Bridgeton, in the East End of Glasgow, where there was no shortage of graduates from what the locals called 'the finishing school' a.k.a. Barlinnie Prison. Tony himself had an uncle who he says, quietly with a chuckle, was a 'muscle man' who 'broke legs' for the Kray twins in London. According to old Joe Gazausis he was not, however, the only mentor Johnny found in the East End and using explosives wasn't the only skill he learned. In the Springfield Road area there was a character called Stankowitz who had a legendary ability to clamber across rooftops in search of lead to steal. Johnny apparently learned a lot from him about the business of scaling the tenement heights in the dark and he took to that like the proverbial duck to water – helped, of course, by his lifelong agility and complete lack of fear of heights.

Tony Russell remembers Johnny with awe bordering on affection. Often he saw him in chapel in Castlemilk on Sunday mornings, though strangely he can't remember Lily accompanying him on these occasions. When not blowing safes or at his devotions Tony remembers Johnny as 'a happy, wild guy' who mellowed later in life. And he remembers him at gatherings in St Luke's, back in town in Ballater Street in the Gorbals, where the Lithuanian community of the East End would often gather for a night's food and old country entertainment. Talking about Johnny, Tony made the by now almost obligatory comment about him always wearing a bunnet or a soft hat. But Tony gave the story a new twist with the observation that he thought it was a habit developed in the old days to hide his prison haircut.

Tony, too, was well aware of Johnny's gambling habit. Tony accompanied him to many of Glasgow's 'flapping tracks' for a night at the dogs. Johnny, it seemed, preferred the likes of Clydebank, Mount Vernon, Partick, Motherwell, Blantyre and Springfield Road to the more genteel attractions of regular tracks like Shawfield, home of Clyde FC at that time, which came under the umbrella of the Greyhound Racing Association.

Apart from the dog tracks, Johnny was a familiar figure at many of Glasgow's dodgy gambling clubs. Tony also confirms that Johnny was a heavy punter who did not dabble in pound bets. His excitement as a punter came from wagering large wads of the folding stuff. On one of these nights at the dogs, Tony found himself in more heavy-duty criminal company than that of Johnny, the safe blower who eschewed violence and did not too often rob the common man. One night at Mount Vernon they ran into a certain Peter Manuel, later identified as Scotland's most infamous mass murderer, who would be executed in the Barlinnie hanging shed by the famous hangman Harry Allen.

It is interesting that old Tony, who spent many hours in Johnny's company, did not consider him boastful about his army adventures. Most of the people who knew Johnny after the war said the same. Maybe that was because Johnny never had to bring the subject up – anyone who met him was usually desperate to hear the truth about the adventures they'd read so much about in the papers and they were more than willing listeners. It was slightly different in prison, where a reputation as a tough guy does no harm to your relations with fellow convicts. So it is not all that surprising to read in his prison records that some governors and head warders warned of a tendency towards bragging about his war record to other prisoners and 'playing the big man'. Governors also warned each other about his tendency to play the jailhouse lawyer at every opportunity. But in these rough notes on his prison years there is often a hint of a sort of reluctant admiration for a famous war hero and legendary offender. With a few notable exceptions his captors tended to like 'Gentle Johnny' though they were not naive about the regular promises to go straight.

Old Tony was upfront with his Ramensky connection, not unnaturally considering his age and the fact he lives in Canada. A much younger man, a reformed Gorbals bad guy who now has a nice little business, understandably didn't want to be named when he told me of his memories of Johnny. In particular, he gave me confirmation of Johnny's truly remarkable physical ability and strength, as mentioned by Freddy Sutherland. A well known figure in the area to this day, our man had mingled with the likes of Jimmy Boyle before he became a reformed character. The transformation of characters such as Boyle and Hugh Collins was, of course, thanks largely to the efforts of the Barlinnie Special Unit. Judged a huge success by reformers, the unit eventually outlived its usefulness and was closed down – though some of its pioneering ways filtered into mainstream prison policy. At the height of its success the unit attracted criticism from some in the Establishment as being a soft touch for hard men.

Mr X remembered Johnny well from his days in the 1960s,

when he divided his time between the Gorbals, Castlemilk and his old haunts in Rutherglen. Johnny was at home in the Gorbals, staying in Lily Mulholland's flat in Eglinton Street and at times in her new ninth-floor home in Queen Elizabeth Square, amid the cluster of high flats and other bits and pieces of new housing, and new pubs that had replaced the dank, rat-infested close-mouths of the age-blackened tenements where Johnny was brought up after his father died and the family moved from Glenboig to the Gorbals.

Mr X took me walkabout to his old haunts across the river from the New Gorbals to Glasgow Green. Our destination was a small but intriguing structure on the banks of the river. Today, people in search of fitness join a health club, pay a hefty monthly fee and pump iron to a background of whichever pop group happens to be in favour at the time. Back then many youngsters in the Gorbals and Bridgeton made their way down to the Green to train on a curious municipal exercise facility. The high iron framework still stands like a pair of giant Victorian goalposts, looked after by the local authorities and painted dark blue. But the swings, chains and iron rings that once hung from the sturdy crossbar are long gone. Here on summer nights the young bucks exercised, almost in the shadow of the new high flats across the Clyde – which have, aptly you might think, a nice view of a distillery on the south bank beyond.

The tearaways, who in those days, fifty years ago or so, used this free outdoor gym, would hoist themselves on the iron rings and climb up the chains with the power of their arms alone. It was a healthy outlet for aggression and energy. They often had an admiring audience of young Gorbals teenage girls. Later, as darkness fell on summer nights, the youngsters, guys and gals, would disappear back across the river to their haunts in the Gorbals in search of entertainment of a different kind in darkened back courts.

The young men, hard men, impressed the watching girls with their feats of athleticism. But the older figure of Johnny

Ramensky, who regularly joined in these ad hoc keep-fit sessions, was held in something like awe when he took to the hoops and chains. He enjoyed displaying his strong arms and his famous agility to the youngsters. His reputation in an area where law-breakers were thick on the ground brought him automatic respect.

Mr X also told me of a demonstration of Johnny's strength and the kindness he often exhibited. One day Johnny and some friends were on a landing in the Gorbals high flats – on something like the fifteenth storey – and a woman arrived with a pushchair and a child. Apparently there was some trouble with the lifts and it was down the stairs on foot or nothing. Two or three of the guys helped Johnny pick up the child and chair and headed downstairs. After a few floors the hard men suddenly lost the notion of playing the Good Samaritan and Johnny was left on his own to slog it to the bottom, carrying the chair and child. This he did, no problem. In one little incident he had shown three of his remarkable traits – kindness, strength and likeability.

That consistent kindness to others is something that his niece Dorothy McNab, a widow for ten years now, remembers as she browses through her mementoes of her famous uncle. In her early teens Dorothy recalls happy days in Regent Street, Rutherglen, when Johnny either stayed with, or popped in to see, his sisters Agnes and Margaret. Johnny and Agnes were in regular contact, closer perhaps after the death of their brother Frank, who died young, and after their other brother Joe emigrated to Canada to make a new life for himself. If Johnny was flush with gambling money – as he sometimes, just sometimes, was – he would lavish affection and cash on his teenage niece. Mind you, it did not always work out the way Dorothy thought. She still laughs how one birthday (her fifteenth) she dreamed of a present of a bike to get her upsides a few lucky pals who pedalled round Rutherglen. It was an unlikely dream for her in those straitened times for families. But Johnny was the famous man, the big man with big pockets, and the man to provide the bike – or so she thought.

A lively woman with a good sense of humour, Dorothy still laughs as she recalls her birthday treat. Johnny took her into town to the famous old Odeon cinema to see *A Star is Born* with Judy Garland and James Mason, and to treat her to a slap-up meal in a city restaurant. So far so good – this was the high life for a wee lassie from Rutherglen. She even entertained the notion that some folk looking at them might think she was glamorous enough to be a swish young woman out on the town with her sugar daddy. A perfect day out was only spoiled by her present – a white duffel coat. 'Who wanted that for their birthday?' Dorothy laughs. She coveted a bike. But her eyes light up as she remembers the fruit, the flowers and the cards on a memorable birthday.

A famous uncle was nice to have around at times. And Johnny did his standing with a favourite relative no harm with his lunchtime visits to Dorothy at work in Templeton's carpet factory overlooking Glasgow Green. He would take her and a bunch of her pals to the nearest City Bakery shop for a free feed. There was obvious affection between the pair of them. It is interesting that Dorothy says that in all the time she knew her uncle, and amid all his travails in the Army and with the law, she never at any time saw him as anything other than a kindly figure who never lost his temper. Looking back, she describes him as fresh, nice-looking guy who had a touch of the James Cagney in his appearance, something others had remarked on. But she also remembers that trait which may have caused him trouble down the years. He was a very generous guy who could spend money as fast as he got it.

Johnny Ramensky was certainly a complex character. He clearly loved Lily very much, enjoyed the company of his relatives and friends and even enjoyed normal life from time to time. But, despite his best intentions, it seems that regular life simply didn't have enough thrills for Johnny and, sooner or later, he would leave the straight and narrow for the crooked path once more. And for Lily, left with her family and to her own devices for so much of her time while her husband languished in jail, life would not be easy. There can be no doubt that this would have put an almost intolerable strain on any relationship.

# 17

# A BOOK BURNING

It would be wrong to give the impression that the tales of happiness and fun in the 1950s and 1960s defined Johnny Ramensky's life in his final decades. These were simply little spikes of normality and freedom for a man who spent more than half his life in jails. Mostly it was business as usual for Johnny – behind bars, and jousting with officialdom in an almost constant stream of letters. It was a habit he had acquired almost from his first experience of jail in the 1920s and it was clearly something he enjoyed. If you are literate, letter-writing is a useful way of passing the long hours of boredom when incarcerated. Small matters such as what sweets and soft drinks can be bought in the canteen with meagre prison earnings take on the gravity of international trade disputes for prisoners with endless time on their hands and access to pen and paper.

You have to feel some sympathy with prison governors who, to this day, have to deal with the endless stream of gripes from those of their charges who have learned how to put a letter of complaint together. And worse still, those who see themselves as jailhouse lawyers. Prisoners don't take no for an answer and one reply follows another, sometimes for months on end. Long correspondences with governors became a habit which Johnny found hard to kick and down the years he spent countless hours petitioning the authorities about his grievances.

One of the complaints that motivated Johnny to pick up his

pen after he was demobbed from the Commandos was his failure as a bookmaker. During his long sentences after the war there was always, at the back of his mind, the notion that when liberated he could get back into the gambling business. And in particular he enjoyed reading the racing pages of the newspapers. He especially revered the old Glasgow *Noon Record*. This was part of the *Daily Record* publishing empire at one time, produced on the same presses in Hope Street, Glasgow, and with its own small dedicated staff, some of whom were themselves keen gamblers desperate to beat the bookies. The *Noon Record* was the bible for the Scottish racing man in the days long before TV racing programmes and the Internet made information a 24/7 option. Designed to take on the national racing papers, like the *Sporting Life,* it did not waste valuable newsprint, or editorial time, on non-racing matters. And for years it had a loyal following for its tipsters, like the famous Silver Ringer, and the up-to-date information from stables and yards it provided.

In Peterhead in the late 1940s, Johnny pleaded desperately for the privilege of reading the racing paper. In those days prisoners had limited access to daily papers, though weeklies were available. But Johnny argued that since he only wanted the *Noon Record* on a Monday, though the paper was a daily, the rule should not apply to him. It was a typical street-smart way of thinking. He wrote, 'I am a bookmaker in civvy street and it is essential I keep in touch with sporting events. If I lose touch with form it would mean a loss of revenue or capital.' He pointed out the unique selling point of the *Noon* – 'it has no public news, but is purely a sporting paper. There are many sporting papers here [in Peterhead], but they are all printed in England with English news. There are no papers here to cater for the Glasgow men.'

In particular he did not like the fact that the *Sunday Mail*, which he was allowed to buy, was the edition for Aberdeen and the north-east. He was more interested in what was going on in Glasgow. He had to have the Monday edition of the *Noon Record* since, 'it is the only paper that can really help me. Monday's paper gives an account of all the sports at the weekend, football, racing and greyhound events.'

There does not appear to be a record of this reasonable request being turned down so the presumption is he got a daily paper one day a week in order to get round the 'no daily papers' rule. Ingenious. But it does not seem to have helped him much as bookie. Long-term, there would be no long coat, white soft hat and big cigar to replace prison garb for this gambler. I suspect that Johnny really only had one winning visit to the bookie – it was said that that's where he met his second wife Lily!

But the letter writing took a turn to more significant matters than racing papers in the 1950s and this time Johnny's pleading was to no avail. He had written to the authorities about taking his life story, written in jail, with him when he left Barlinnie. It culminated in a sad scene, which should rest heavily on the consciences of the officials involved if any are still alive. In the boiler room of the Government Office Building, Broomhouse, Edinburgh on 24 March 1951, K. M. Hancock and G. Wilson signed off a report that said that, in their presence, 'Twenty-six notebooks in their entirety and one notebook from page five onwards were placed in the furnace in this building at 10.30am.' Ultimately, responsibility for this crime of book-burning rested with the then Scottish Secretary, Hector McNeil. These note-books had been taken from Johnny Ramensky, much against his will, on his release from Barlinnie three months earlier. He had only been allowed to keep the handful of his notebooks that dealt with his war service. Officialdom noted of the burning: 'The final stages of the Ramsay incident passed off without any hitch. We must now put our house in order.'

What went up in smoke that spring day in Edinburgh was the Ramensky story in his own words, around a quarter of a million of them. It was the official destruction of an immensely valuable record, written by a man with real communication skills, and something that might have given historians insight into prison and social conditions in the last century. But up in smoke it all went. At the time there were suspicions that Johnny's memoirs contained criticism of senior police figures and of politicians. We will now never know for sure. However, there is no denying that what was burned that day in Edinburgh was the real inside story of a unique life of crime.

One of the reasons that it fell foul of the authorities was because it contained much detail on crimes for which Johnny was never prosecuted. No one in authority liked the idea of the public reading of his undiscovered crimes. Or knowing how many such episodes there were. And there was speculation on what the press would do with the story of undetected crimes and police failures. Johnny seems unworried about the possibility of being charged with offences mentioned in his diary which he had got away with. Maybe he was of the opinion that some of his claims would be too hard for the cops to prove after the event. In any event this episode was the culmination of a lifetime of effort by Johnny to put his story down on paper. Even in the 1930s he was secretly keeping notes but his attempt to write a full-blown life story started in earnest in Peterhead in 1951. The governor, Major D.C. Heron-Watson, seems to have given him permission to write his story despite the fact that in Scottish prisons generally, at that time, there was confusion about whether it was permissible to allow prisoners to make money from crimes on release.

Although he had started writing in Peterhead, Johnny's epic story was completed in Barlinnie. Before a decision was reached on what to do with his notebooks they were given to the governor to read. He reported that: 'They are well written in a concise and straightforward manner and the few grammatical and spelling errors could be easily put right.' The review of Johnny's scribblings went on to say: 'It is interesting and in parts exciting and there is no doubt Ramsay could get a fair amount of money from a newspaper such as the *News of the World* whose representatives have already interviewed him.' Surprisingly, a newspaperman had been allowed into Peterhead to see him earlier, so there can have been no clear policy on how best to deal with such issues.

The report went on: 'His description of his early days in Glasgow shows how it is almost inevitable that a youngster in his circumstances, and with a penchant for gambling, should drift into crime. His exploits in the Commandos in the war show him in a good light and I doubt that the War Office could object to publication of this part of his story. His experiences in prison in the main, without over-drawing the picture, and his detailed account of his escapes from Peterhead, make interesting reading.'

That was the good news but the report went on: 'Then we move to his burglary adventures – houses, offices, factories, shops, quite often in the company of criminals from England, Scotland and Wales. This bit included confessions of crimes he got away with. It mentions Glasgow fences and his comments on the Glasgow police far from flatter. Not a good idea to let this stuff out.'

The Governor went on to say: 'I have formed the impression that Ramsay will never reform. Gambling and safe blowing are in his blood. He does not come into the category of the "shilling each way" punter. He gets a thrill out of gambling hundreds of pounds.' This report ended with the observation that Johnny had no regrets and would do it all again. It also suggests that the authorities should follow the English example of the time and not allow prisoners to write their stories when inside. It recommends refusing Johnny permission to take his notebooks out with him, other than the war material. Reading this file in the Scottish National Archives, it is clear that the writer had a grudging admiration for Johnny and knew that not to give him the notebooks would be a 'big blow to him' emotionally. And it would lose him money.

That observation was correct. Johnny was furious at what he called the suppression of his work. And he made a powerful point: he said that in writing the work he had been, 'fair and generous in my approach. After all I could have written about brutality and villainy, which I witnessed in every prison I was in. Warders can be merciless. Give me back my notebooks.' Like his frequent court appeals for one last chance, this plea, which now feels totally justified, fell on deaf ears. So that appears to have been that and the authorities got their way.

Johnny blew a bit hot and cold with the press, sometimes cooperating with newspapers – to help finance his marriage to Lily, for example – at other times taking a more distant stance. An example of this comes in a letter to a reporter, Norman Rae of the *News of the World*, and it gives a striking insight into his thinking. He wrote to the newsman at the paper's headquarters in Bouverie Street, London, in reply to an offer from the journalist to help him write his stories:

I am sorry I can not meet with your wishes. I believe I owe you an explanation. So here it is. I am a crook, always have been and there is no turning back. My heart is in the game and I would not have it otherwise. When I started to write my life story I did so to while away some idle moments. My intention was to have the book published when I reached seventy or after my death. The financial reward from the book means very little to me, because I know from experience that money, even big money, makes no difference to my mode of life.

The game is what matters. What chance would I have travelling round the town on business with my photograph blazoned for months on the pages of a Sunday newspaper? The public would hasten to identify me as soon as a safe was done. And some crackpot would identify me in places I had never been. No, sir, my liberty is too precious to be lost that way. The notoriety of recent days will be forgotten in 1954 and I will only have the police to worry about. So financially what I lose on the swings I gain on the roundabouts. I would temper my refusal with the assurance that offers from other

newspapers would get the same answer. Each man has an ambition and I have fulfilled mine years ago. I cherish my career as a safe blower. In childhood days my feet were planted on the crooked path and took firm root. To each one of us is allotted a niche and I have found mine. Strangely enough I am happy. The die is cast and for me there is no turning back. It is with regret that I refuse your generous offer. Yours, very sincerely,
John Ramsay.

This must be one of the most remarkable letters ever written by a prisoner in a Scottish jail. The acceptance of the permanence of his way of life and the price he had to pay for it is total. It is the letter of a highly intelligent man facing facts, in particular the fact that by now, his war record notwithstanding, it was impossible for him to go straight. And in any case he did not want to do that. His situation is expressed in almost poetic terms but all this philosophy did not mean he could not change his mind on some things. His fear that his photo in the paper would hinder his career as a cat burglar is overstated – after all he had been on the front pages for years. Few who read the papers could not put a name to the often-used wartime snap of him smiling in his Commando Green Beret. And every cop on the beat had seen his face smiling out of the *Police Gazette*. Like it or not he was a criminal celebrity, recognised wherever he went.

In the end, in the 1960s, he talked extensively to various reporters and newspapers about his career in return for cash. He was still in the 'game' but the old worry about getting his picture in the paper had been laid aside in a pragmatic understanding that his infamy could help pay the rent, if not his gambling debts. In his dealings with Norman Rae, a big name in his day in newspaper circles, he showed both something of his literary abilities and a genuine respect for the man trying to get a story for his paper. Letter-writing came easy to Johnny, with his epistles written in a clear firm hand with few spelling or punctuation errors. At school with those 'urchins' in the Gorbals, whom he alleges led him astray all those years ago, he must at least have had a good English teacher. Especially when you consider that some family members spoke only Lithuanian. If nothing else, he was a good learner.

# 18

# LOVE LETTERS

When a man puts pen to paper to write about his life he opens a window into his soul and gives insight into the changes the years bring. Johnny's many letters from the 1950s and 1960s point to a gradual change in character as his career was drawing to a close. Maybe the constant false dawns and failed 'new starts', one after another, which were always washed away by his repeated offending, were beginning to hurt. As, perhaps, was his growing understanding of his own character. Added to this was the fact that by now he was beginning to lose his legendary fitness and agility.

He was still a cat burglar, but a sometimes stiff and aging one in a young man's game. So it is not all that surprising that the 'likeable rogue' of civvy street could have fallings out from time to time with fellow prisoners looking to show the old man that he was past it and that there were new kids on the block.

One sad episode in particular caused him a delay in returning to the welcoming arms of his Lily. It came about because of a spat with an ex-cop and was the reason for one of his escapes, in 1952. At the time he had a cushy job as an orderly in the prison hospital but trouble with one of his charges in the ward led to an increase in his sentence. Poor Lily Mulholland must have never known what news the postman would deliver from the jail-house from one day to the next. Or what the headlines might be about Johnny in the morning papers.

His escapes must have been particularly tense times for her – when he was inside she at least knew where he was. When he was on the run anything could have happened to him. A letter explaining the reason for one of his many escapes, and why he would be longer away from her fireside than expected, is particularly poignant. It also shows a shortening fuse in his dealings with fellow inmates, something to his credit that he did not shy away from or try to hide. There is always a direct honesty in his letters.

On this occasion he wrote to his 'dear Lily':

This is me, yes me. I know you will be wondering what went wrong with me [a reference to the headlines on his escape]. I told you I was happy at my work. I said the same thing to others and I even believed it myself. But I did not allow for a cantankerous old copper who was sent for protection to the hospital to serve his two years. We had many bitter arguments and on Sunday night last he complained I had assaulted him with the result I was put on report to face the Governor in the morning.

The effect of this caused me some worry and the thought of losing my hospital job upset me. Instead of keeping the heid, as I should have done, I recklessly resolved to run away. So during the early hours I broke out, but without any plans or ideas of what I wanted, but the urge to run away from it all. But it is not easy to run away from trouble, as I should have known. Only more trouble piles up and that is how it is now. I will be punished in a few days and maybe I will be unable to write to you for some time. Don't worry about me – whatever punishment comes my way I will be able to take it. After all they must feed me something and as regards other matters I will manage along. I am sorry love I am such a worry to you, but honestly dear, I could not help it. The impulse was too strong to resist so I fell for it. What is for you won't go past you. I am sorry dear only for your sake.
Love John.

Johnny was right to surmise that this business would cost him some remission time. And it did. Many months. So he had some explaining to do to Lily. He continued to make his apologies in another letter, this time even more affectionate than his previous occasionally flowery efforts. He wrote:

I am sorry dear for your sake that I lost so much time because we were so much looking forward to being together. We were so happy and I never dreamed at the way events would change so swiftly. I really believed I would be home in June. I really hope Lily that you wont be too angry with me for my foolishness, as I never dreamed such a thing would happen. Will you tell Tommy [Clark] the bad news as soon as you can, because he is always enquiring? I will do my best to forget this unhappy episode and build my dreams around the day in December when I can hold you again. I love you so much that you are constantly in my thoughts. It is a shame that you should suffer and very unfair of me. All I can say Lily is that I hope to make it up some day. I think the world of the family and I feel I have let them down. I love them very much and like to read about their doings in your letters. Dear Lily forgive me for my faults, because I love you so much, God bless you dear.
John.

These are the words of a man besotted with an attractive woman who had fallen hard for him. In her frequent appearances in the press, in her role as 'the woman who waits for her man', her red hair and beauty are almost always mentioned by the scribes. But, the occasional burst of publicity apart, it was a hard life being Mrs John Ramsay. Reading the love letter above you would imagine that on release from his current, extended, sentence he would never put Lily through such emotional turmoil again. You would be wrong. Several years later Johnny was back behind bars, unable to leave the crooked path.

The only consolation for Lily was that at least he had been transferred to Barlinnie and the long slog north to Peterhead for a few words through a glass screen was no longer necessary. The train fare was £4, quite a sum in these days, too much for Lily and she encouraged Johnny to work for a transfer south which he eventually got. In a year he got four half-hour visits. Lily told a Sunday paper reporter that she got the first half hour all to herself and the other visits were shared with Johnny's family.

Johnny's long record and his often proven ability as a jail-breaker meant that at this time he was on the Bar-L 'A List' as a potential escaper. He was subject to all sorts of little deprivations not endured by trusties who kept their head down and ticked off the days to liberation. However, his return to Barlinnie was at least a step forward and Lily told all and sundry how much she looked forward to their visits in the forbidding surroundings of the 'big hoose' in the East End of Glasgow. It was a marriage and a life that many in Glasgow understood. But still a far from conventional one.

# 19

# HEADING FOR A FALL

Even as the years started to catch up with Johnny, his work was mostly solitary. For a man at the centre of the crime world, in a city infamous worldwide for its gangs, it is interesting that Johnny was never a 'gangster'. He was his own man. If one of the city's many godfathers was puzzled about how to bust a safe filled with readies, he would call on Johnny as the undoubted expert. Johnny never let them down. But he never ran in a group with Glasgow's hard men.

The only working relationships he had through the years were with a succession of 'powder monkeys' – his assistants on jobs. These guys, like his brother-in-law Mario de Marco, and his old mate, wee Tommy Clark, took part in many a safe blowing. Their role was to pass the ammunition to the safe blower, keep a look out, help carry the gear and generally assist the brains of the operation in his work. In the early 1960s this role was played for Johnny by a Greenock man called Tony Salmon – the two had met in Barlinnie. Tony was a dab hand at helping with the explosive but had the added advantage of being a skilled locksmith. Picking difficult locks and manufacturing keys from stolen dummies were meat and drink to him. So skilled were some of these locksmiths that they could memorise the pattern of a key at a single viewing and without any other aids manufacture a replica which did the job.

The number of Johnny's crimes may run to hundreds of jobs

over the years. He was always restlessly active at his trade. The only source that could take us anywhere near to the knowing the actual number of crimes he got away with unfortunately went up in smoke in that government furnace in Edinburgh. It was certainly a figure large enough to scare those in authority, who feared what the newspapers and the general public would make of it. And you have to presume his memoirs would only record the crimes he thought were of particular interest. Many would go unrecorded, even by him.

In the outside world, Lily was a constant supporter who would fight Johnny's cause constantly. She fought to get him transferred to a jail nearer home, to better his conditions and, when Johnny was in Aberdeen prison in the late 1960s she had a remarkable battle with the authorities to get him parole. It was a one-woman fight – Johnny himself did not ask for early release. It seems he knew that with his infamy, his huge number of previous convictions and his ability to escape when stressed out in jail that he had no chance. His reluctance to help Lily in her fight may have been caused by a desire not to get her hopes up in a vain quest. It may also have been down, at least in part, to his growing institutionalisation. Lily herself, as mentioned earlier, even called prison his 'second home'. The brave man of the war, unafraid of anything the Nazis could throw at him and equally unafraid of the cops who constantly watched his movements when free, was perhaps now fearful of freedom itself. It must have sunk into his consciousness that when free he could feel trapped by the everyday realities of life. He wanted the best for Lily, but despite his talk he always seemed to let her down. Sitting alone in his cell that thought must have hurt him. Would it be any different if he got parole? Was he scared to face the responsibilities of freedom and earning an honest living?

At this time Lily had problems galore of her own. Her health had never been all that good and she had long-term chest problems. Also in 1968, when in Eglinton Street, she lost her home in one of the most spectacular natural disasters in Scottish history. Glasgow's Great Storm, as it became known, made 2,000 people homeless. Lily was one of them – the winter hurricane winds damaged the tenement property she stayed in so badly that it had to be demolished. Glasgow was forced to spend millions repairing buildings ravaged by wind and rain. This, in a way, was not to be deplored, for before the Great Storm many of dwellings, particularly in the poorer areas, were to say the least sub-standard, some barely fit to live in. Lily ended up on the ninth floor of one of new high flats in the Gorbals in what was called a 'spinster' flat with a combined living room/bedroom, kitchen and bathroom. It was hardly luxurious, but at least it was bright and modern.

The new house would not have been suitable for Johnny to share with her had she managed to get him parole. But that was not a problem because the housing department of the time would have looked favourably on an exchange, raising the possibility of a nice house in a suburb or one of the newer schemes.

Lily made a good impression with the authorities, even if Johnny was regarded with some cynicism, and one probation officer investigating the request for parole remarked that her family relationships were good: 'Mrs Ramsay is frank and apparently sincere, she is most anxious to have her husband considered for parole and it is felt at this stage she may be an asset in any future rehabilitation programme. She corresponds and visits regularly. If he got parole she says she could get him a job with a demolition company.' This would have been an ideal job for Johnny with his knowledge of explosives and head for heights. The danger inherent in tearing down big buildings would have also appealed to him.

Lily had worked as a popular waitress in the elite Southside golf club, Haggs Castle, for ten years, testimony to her reliability and ability to earn for herself. Some of Johnny's friends may have felt she regarded him as a meal ticket – an odd masculine view since most of the time he was in jail. There is some irony, too, in the fact that while Lily was ironing her waitress uniform and plodding across Glasgow to the plush Haggs dining room to distribute well-done steaks and perhaps a drop of claret to the members, her husband was supping meagre prison fare. Lily had a relative who worked for the building firm Bovis who would have taken her husband on the payroll, as would Sam B. Allison, the doyen of demolition in the city. But he spurned these opportunities to put the past behind him.

An assessment of Johnny's character at the time noted: 'Mellowed with the years, he is cooperative, quiet and well behaved. And when the occasion demands he can be a steadying influence on more explosive types.' You presume there was no joke intended in this description! The report added, 'It was thought that with some help and guidance from his wife he may go straight.'

It was a hugely optimistic observation considering the facts of his life to that stage. And in the end the authorities ruled 'no parole', confirming Johnny's realistic belief that he had gone down that crooked path too long to change. Johnny had certainly not fooled all of the folk who examined the plea for parole. The official report said of him: 'This person's pleasing personality could easily lead one to suggest he has given up crime. Unfortunately there is no positive indication of this. Though he may mean well there are some signs that he still, to some extent, enjoys the notoriety of his past exploits.'

So the faceless bureaucrats, so often at the end of press criticisms, seem to have got it right this time. Perhaps it could be said that even Johnny himself welcomed the decision which meant he did not have to face the pressure of constant good behaviour and striving not to let a good woman down.

This time round, Johnny had some more years to wait before he was back in Glasgow and back in the old routine of 'housebreaking with intent to steal' as the courts had it. Another botched crime in 1970 got Johnny back in the headlines. Not only was this, his second-last job, a spectacular failure, it almost cost him his life. It certainly contributed to his death in Perth Prison and a significant change in him in his final years. The old Gentle Johnny Ramensky, the gallus, daring safe blower, the likeable rogue of legend, was already no more.

# 20

# GAME OVER

Like all so-called master criminals, Johnny spent time planning robberies and picking juicy targets. That was part of the fun, part of the game. You had homework to do and sometimes even a wee recce in daylight before you pulled on the gloves, worked out what type of 'gelly' to use, and the correct amount, packed the fuses and the wires and timers into the tool bag and set out on a midnight rendezvous with excitement. His selection of what would be his second-last job seemed good, at least on paper. This time there were two targets. The first was the Stirling Burgh factor's office (formerly the Burgh court) where there was around four grand in rent money in the safe. Adjoining this building was the Crown Inn, a popular howff where there would surely be plenty of cash in used notes in the safety of a locked till. It would be a two-pronged attack and his Commando training must have stood him in good stead in the planning. It was the execution that went badly wrong.

This time the great explosives expert was having an off-form night, as had happened in Main Street, Rutherglen, a few years before. Two charges were detonated and the noise was such that neighbours of the Crown Inn called the cops. They arrived at the Crown to see a hole hacked in a ceiling, a rope dangling from rafters, tools and bits and pieces of explosives scattered around the floor. There was no sign of Johnny, but in the silence of the night there was a disturbing moaning sound coming from the car park. Johnny had seemingly realised that the sound of the botched explosion would attract the cops and he had climbed back up his rope in an attempt to flee. Out on the rooftop he could not jouk around in his usual agile way – his age saw to that – and there is speculation that he leapt at a rone pipe in order to slide back to earth. The 'rone pipe' appears to have been merely a dark shadow on the side of the wall, not solid iron that could take him to safety. This theory is given validity by the fact that Johnny had cataract trouble which impaired his once exceptional night vision. He plummeted around sixty feet onto the concrete below.

As he lay moaning in severe pain, he was still making a futile attempt to hide explosives and fuse wire that were in his possession from the police who stood over him. His injuries were extensive – a fractured skull, thigh and wrist – and he spent fourteen weeks in Stirling Infirmary. Eventually, when he did appear in court, it was in a wheelchair. Pleas in mitigation from his defence team made much of the fact that he was now a 'broken man'. To anyone who saw him and knew him this seems a fair description. His physical powers had been on the wane for some time. Years of prison food, lacking the vitamins a man needs, had taken their toll. These days dieticians and prison medics make sure that even the most evil and unreformable old lags get a rounded diet. Johnny had had to endure years eating poor-quality food, fed to him by people who would have been shocked at any attempt to give prisoners a decent diet. Indeed Johnny was something of a pioneer in pointing out to the authorities how such diets made prisoners fall sick and even die, from illnesses that most people out on the streets would take in their stride.

Reading the menus of these days brings home that point – tea, bread and marge, potatoes and an apple or orange once in a blue moon are not conducive to good health. But for many years, before it caught up with him, he survived. Indeed, his old friend Governor Duncan Mackenzie, around a decade before this trial, said he was the fittest man he had ever known.

Be that as it may, in the Stirling trial the prosecution and others, perhaps influenced by the legend of the great escaper, were more hard-nosed than the newspapers. Their picture of the man in the dock was not the reality of someone seriously ill and aging prematurely. The power of his legend suggested to them that he was resilient enough to recover and perhaps return to criminal ways. Whatever the state of his health, he was on the way back to prison, first to the Bar-L, then transferred to Perth.

The notes that went with him to Perth, a place where he had never been incarcerated before, described him as separated from Lily – all the anguish in their relationship had finally taken its toll. His last few months of freedom had been spent with his sister Agnes. After the trial he was said to have been working in buckle production in the Glasgow prison, earning 40p a week, before his transfer to Perth. There were no 'welfare or protection' problems. Another note, this time compiled in Perth, again said he was married but separated and working in the mailbag repair party. His conduct and industry were described as good and the report continued: 'This is the well known John Ramsay, escaper extraordinary. Though perhaps past his best in this field he may prove to be a jailhouse lawyer.'

Warders and governors get to know their charges well. Even in the few months before his death Johnny was still at the letter-writing. This time it was a small squabble with the Lanarkshire police over clothes taken from him on arrest and allegedly not returned. He completed the time given to him for the Stirling job but the cynics at that trial who thought he would offend again were absolutely right.

His last arrest occurred in Ayr where, in 1972, he was found hiding behind a chimneystack on a rooftop. A sad touch here is that he had been nabbed before he could even steal a penny and the final charge came under the Prevention of Crimes Act. He was on deferred sentence from Edinburgh Sheriff Court at the time. He had been seen on the roof by members of the public and was arrested by two policemen who had climbed up after him. There was no place to hide, no spurious defence plea.

Despite a guilty plea, his lawyer, the famous Joe Beltrami, was yet again pressed by his client to use his remarkable skills as a pleader to influence the judge to show some leniency. Joe knew that Johnny's age and obvious ill health meant that a maximum sentence would mean his client was likely to die in jail. He decided bringing a bit of humour to the proceedings might help. He told the bench and the court with a smile that Mr Ramsay had been on more roofs than the now famous Fiddler. Laughter in court, up to a point. But the judge did not seem unduly amused or affected by the plea and the old rascal was handed down his last sentence. He was jailed for a year, and a deferred six-month sentence was added at Edinburgh Sheriff Court six months later.

Johnny was on his way to Perth prison and a reunion with Willie 'Sonny' Leitch in Scotland's oldest prison, a daunting structure even today, built originally in the early nineteenth century to hold French prisoners captured during the Napoleonic Wars. Johnny spent his final hours in one of the five halls, 'C' Hall, a forbidding place which was knocked down in 2006. It was a distressing place for the final illness of a man who had lost his supreme physical fitness in a slow decline behind bars that could not be halted even with the regular keep-fit regime he did his best to stick to in jail.

Even in death there was controversy. This centred on how quickly Johnny was taken to hospital. This is truly ironic, taking into account the number of 'petitions' he himself had delivered to the authorities on the treatment of prisoners who fall ill. The official report of what happened that fateful day in 1972 is deadpan. It tells the events as follows:

Ramsay was employed in the pool party on fairly light work. On Friday November 3 a prison officer noted that the prisoner was not very well and immediately advised the surgery. At approximately 2pm nursing officer Hammond visited Ramsay in the party. The nursing officer immediately returned him to his cell and put him to bed. Thereafter the prisoner was frequently observed by the hall staff. At approximately four it was reported to the surgery that Ramsay was unwell. The nursing officer examined him and called the senior nursing officer who immediately notified the medical officer at 4.20. Dr Moffat arrived, examined the patient and authorised his immediate removal to Perth Royal Infirmary. Prisoner was transferred by ambulance (accompanied by a nursing officer) at 4.55pm. At 4.55 Rutherglen Police were notified with the request they notify the prisoner's next of kin, Mrs Milliken of Rutherglen [his sister Agnes]. Contact was maintained with Perth Infirmary and throughout Sat Nov 4 the prisoner's condition was assessed as very poor. We were advised that Mrs Milliken had visited the hospital on Saturday. [She found that Johnny was simply 'just done'.] At approximately 9.30pm the hospital reported the prisoner had died. On Sunday Nov 5 inquiries were received from the Scottish Information Organisation. A member of Mrs Ramsay's family had phoned and expressed surprise that the widow had not been informed. It was explained that her address was not available to us and that the prisoner had given his next of kin as Mrs Milliken. It was arranged that Mrs Ramsay would get in touch with Mrs Milliken to come to some arrangement about the funeral arrangements. On Monday November 6 Mrs Ramsay and her son, Mr Main, visited the hospital to uplift the death certificate. I acquainted Mrs Ramsay with the circumstances of her husband's death and informed the cause of death as cerebral haemorrhage.

The fact that Johnny and Lily were separated in his final years is sad but all too predictable. Not all of Johnny's criminal pals ever really took to Lily. One told me that he thought that she was a bit too keen to spend Johnny's money when he was flush and there was a suspicion that maybe to him she was a touch of what is today called 'arm candy'. But the records show that down the years she fought hard for her man, writing endless letters about parole requests, prison transfers and trying hard to help him get a new life out of jail and on the straight and narrow. It was a hopeless task and no doubt she finally came to the same conclusion as Johnny's sometime defender in court, Joe Beltrami, that Johnny had a compulsion both to break into places where excitement and money could be found and a similar compulsion to break out when incarcerated. The one final certainty in his life was that it would continue in the sad circle of a crime followed by imprisonment followed at the end of a sentence with the declaration that from now on he would go straight.

But it would, of course, be inappropriate to describe this as a vicious circle in Lily's case. Marriage to such a man brought some happy days but many more unhappy ones, bringing up a family alone while the love of her life rotted in jail. You can't help feeling that any of the little episodes of happiness in Lily's life with Gentle Johnny were deserved. Being Mrs Johnny Ramensky and raising a family while working regularly as a waitress was no easy life.

The reports of Johnny's final hours in the archives are, by their nature, somewhat detached, though the feeling that Johnny was to an extent liked and admired by his warders does shine through even the civil service style. However, much more human and touching is the account of his final hours as told by Willie Leitch. We sat together in a Lanarkshire pub as he recalled what had happened the day he lost a man who had become, over the years, a close friend. Willie Leitch is not, one suspects, an over-emotional man, but the retelling of Johnny's last hours affected him.

The day Johnny took ill had, as the official report made clear, begun like any other. One difference was that in Perth, and any other jail, a Friday is different from other days. The weekend approaches and with it a change of routine. No one is going outside the high walls that shut the criminals off from normality. There is no looking forward to a spot of golf or a trip to watch the local football team, St Johnstone, in action. But there would be a little break in the monotony – perhaps a film (in the days before TVs became part of cell furniture) a visit to the prison church, or maybe some extra time on the sports field.

So there was a somewhat cheery atmosphere in the 'pool party engaged on fairly light work' as the official report described it. The light work was that somewhat clichéd occupation of prison life – working on mailbags. Sewing mailbags is something of prison legend, but Johnny, Willie and friends were not working on seams or patching bags that day. Their task was to fix metal tabs round the openings on the hessian sacks so that the Post Office sorters could hook them up on to pegs on the stands used to move the sacks around the sorting office.

The work on the mailbags was not exactly brain-stretching and the prisoners that morning were playing the old prison game of 'Wordie' to keep the grey matter active while doing the mind-bendingly boring work that they faced day after day. Little slips of paper were passed between the toilers and each wrote a letter on the slip. The prisoners then tried to form words from the letters. It was a primitive form of the popular board game Scrabble, without the need for a board or tiles marked with the letters. I remarked to Willie that Johnny would be a natural winner at this, given his talent in jailhouse lawyer work. 'You'd be surprised,' said the old lag. 'There were plenty of clever folk in Perth then!'

But soon it was obvious that Johnny was not enjoying this particular game of 'Wordie'. He had been complaining for some time of bad headaches. And this particular morning he kept rubbing his forehead over one of his eyes. Johnny put this down to the after-effects of a whack with a police baton on one of his many arrests. But the last time Willie saw him it seemed that what was troubling his friend was more than a little headache. He was continually rubbing his head and according to Willie,

'There was a big red patch moving across the side of his face and one eye appeared bloodshot.' At this stage the guys in the work party were worried about him, though he insisted he was all right, as you do. But the cons wanted him looked at and a warder was summoned. Sandy Bain, a well-known warder who had seen service as a pilot in the war, came to have a look.

It was decided to take Johnny back to his cell, though the pass men were told to keep it unlocked so that the 'screws' could keep an eye on him. The prison surgery was also involved. In the cell he seemed confused, talking to himself, and was bleeding from the mouth, perhaps as a result of biting himself in minor convulsions. After a while he was at the cell door, virtually naked, except for a pair of trainers, and telling anyone who would listen that he was going to the pictures. This lack of dress was not at all Johnny's style, says Willie. Even in prison he liked to be neat. Those trainers he wore also told something of the man. They actually belonged to Willie Leitch, who had tried to give them to Johnny as a gift. This proud man would have none of that, so in a little subterfuge Willie asked him to wear them 'to break them in for me'. By now it was clear that Johnny was really ill and shortly after this appearance at his cell door he was on his way to Perth Royal Infirmary.

Around twenty-four hours later, word came back to the men of Perth that he had died in hospital. Johnny was a figure held in great respect by his fellow prisoners, and it can be said, by many of his warders. Saturday night in any prison can be a noisy place. Particularly because the young Turks, used to Saturday night excitement out on the streets, can use this as an excuse for a verbal rammy, shouting to each other and rattling their cages, generally making as much noise as possible, and being awkward with the warders. The news of the death of Gentle John Ramensky altered all that. That Saturday night the great echoing halls of the prison lay silent. 'Even the mice must have known something had happened,' says Willie.

A few days after Johnny's death, a notice appeared on the boards of Perth's various halls to the effect that, 'A collection was made on behalf of the late John Ramsay. The amount collected was £24.40. The wreath which was forwarded on your behalf cost £5.10 and the balance of £19.30 has been forwarded to his wife by cheque.' Glasgow's two main sources of local news reported the death, but not in the extravagant terms that would be used now with double-page spreads and feature writers recording his astonishing life. The *Record* baldly reported: 'Time Runs Out for Gentle Johnny' with a report a few paragraphs in length pushed back to page twelve in a paper more concerned about politicians freezing wages and the doings of Idi Amin in far-off Africa.

One of Johnny's old foes, Detective Chief Superintendent James Binnie, was quoted as saying, 'He was the type of man for whom you had to have a certain respect and fondness.' The *Herald*, in its then usual deadpan style, had an equally short report headed 'Death of John Ramensky'. Later the feature articles and the tributes to his war service were to appear regularly in the papers.

One of those not at the funeral, arranged by Agnes Milliken and Lily, was Willie Leitch, who languished in HMP Perth as the remains of his friend were laid to rest in St Kentigern's cemetery in Lambhill, Glasgow, after a funeral mass in the Southside. The funeral was notable for the fact that it was attended by almost as many policemen as family and friends – some of those friends on the wrong side of the law. The press also noted that there was a sprinkling of English accents in the congregation and some smartly dressed men who, it was suggested, would not have looked out of place in, shall we say, Whitehall.

The final resting place of Johnny Ramensky in Lambhill is today a melancholy place, his stone cross lying on its side, on an incline littered with similar toppled stones; a vast and vandalised area reeking of dereliction and sadness. There is little to indicate that here lies one of the most remarkable Scots of the twentieth century, a man some called a common criminal yet who managed to capture the public's imagination and affection. And a man who played an extraordinary role in the fight against the Nazis.

Maybe it is as a Commando that his great-grandson and great-granddaughter think most of him when they visit the funereal desolation of St Kentigern's. Young Haig Ferguson and his sister Kendal are proud of their famous relative. Kendal in particular has spent much time in recent years retracing his career. Dorothy McNab says that her Uncle John enjoyed the company of young folk. I suspect he would have been proud of Haig and Kendal. Maybe his shadow was not too far away a few years ago when Kendal, as a fourteen-year-old, addressed her schoolmates in Greenfaulds High, a stark modern building in the somewhat dispiriting new town of Cumbernauld. The teacher had asked the class to prepare an address to deliver to their mates on someone they admired, or someone famous. It was low-key classroom training in the art of speaking in public. The girls in her class mostly spoke of pop stars or sporting personalities. Kendal proudly told of the astonishing career of her great-grandfather. Few had heard of him, but they listened in rapt attention as Kendal told them the legend of Johnny Ramensky.

On his eventual release from prison, Willie Leitch went on a pilgrimage, not to Lambhill, but to a spot high on a Highland hill. There, at the magnificent Commando memorial at Spean Bridge, one of the most powerful and most visited pieces of public sculpture in Scotland, he laid a little card of his own in honour of his friend. No doubt not long after he had reverently placed it at the base of the monument, the cold, cruel winter wind which blows almost constantly at this spectacular site, would snatch the flimsy cardboard tribute and blow it into the wilderness, into the very hills where an ex-con from a mining village in Lanarkshire learned his craft as a Commando. A craft that for a few years led him away from that 'crooked path' he wrote about so emotionally and transformed him, for a time, into a brave patriot.

Thousands of folk every year flock to the memorial, some family and friends of the Green Berets who died in war devastated Europe. They are on a pilgrimage to show respect to brave men who laid down their lives for their country, the ultimate sacrifice. Others, ordinary tourists from many parts of the world, who have perhaps never heard of a Commando, are drawn to leave the beautiful scenery of the rugged A82 trunk road a few miles north of Spean Bridge by a glimpse from the roadside of this spectacular work of art. The three bronze figures of Commandos look out from their stone plinth to the peaks of the Western Highlands. In the hinterland of these great mountains the Commandos trained, as no other group of soldiers trained, in all-out war. Whatever their reason for being there, today's visitors mostly linger long at the seventeen-foot-high sculpture designed by Scott Sutherland and unveiled by Queen Elizabeth, the Queen Mother in September, 1952. It is a most remarkable piece of work. The memorial has a curious hypnotic quality. As you wander round it, the juxtaposition of the soldiers and the mountains create a series of memorable scenes, each step producing a slightly different view, each one as dramatic as the next. The figures of the soldiers themselves, gazing out to Ben Nevis, are strikingly realistic and powerful.

It is a place that makes you think deeply and reflect on life in the twentieth century. The plaques bolted on to the stone take time to read. Immediately at the feet of the three powerful figures is engraved the Commando's motto 'United We Conquer'. And a plaque states, 'In memory of the officers and men of the Commandos who died in the Second World War 1939–1945. This country was their training ground.' A second plaque, more eloquent, was added to the memorial on the occasion of the Freedom of Lochaber being conferred on the Commando Association in November 1993. It reads:

In the summer of 1940, when Britain's fortunes in World War II were at their lowest ebb and an enemy invasion threatened, Winston Churchill boldly ordered the raising of an elite force to raid the enemy-held coastline of Europe and regain the initiative. The new units, which initially consisted of volunteers from the regiments and corps of the British Army, were called 'Commandos'. Within weeks they were in action in Europe and later in the Middle and Far East. During the next five years they fought in every theatre of war with such success that the word 'Commando' became feared by the enemy – yet respected by friendly forces.

In 1942 the Commando Basic Training Centre was established in the Scottish Highlands at Achnacarry. The potential Commando soldiers (who by then came not only from the British Army but also the Royal Marines and the Allied Armies) underwent their tough and purposeful training. Only those who successfully completed the course were accepted and privileged to wear the Green Beret. This distinctive headdress was acknowledged as the hallmark of the highest standards of military training, self-discipline, physical endurance, initiative, bravery and courage whilst under their simple motto United We Conquer a comradeship beyond literary description was born, fostered and flourished.

For their valour in action Commandos earned thirty eight-battle honours and many awards including eight Victoria Crosses, but many made the supreme sacrifice, no fewer than 1,700 Commando soldiers lost their lives and others were seriously wounded. It was a record that prompted Winston Churchill to pay the following tribute to the Commandos: 'We may feel sure that nothing of which we have any knowledge or record has ever been done by mortal men which surpasses their feats of arms. Truly we may say of them, when shall their glory fade.'

As Willie Leitch gazed at the sculpture and remembered the moving story of his friend, and that immortal band of brothers in khaki, he was much moved. This hillside, swept by wild winds, was a million miles and a million years away from the time he had spent with John Ramsay banged up in Scotland's prisons. As he contemplated his friendship with Johnny, Willie savoured a secret thought. He thinks that one of the faces in the striking trio of Commandos in action gear has a curious resemblance to Yonus Ramanauckas a.k.a. Johnny Ramensky a.k.a. John Ramsay. It is not a totally outrageous suggestion. The sculptor was an Army man and in his military career met many Commandos. That rugged, slightly pugilistic profile of Johnny is certainly typical of the determination of the Commandos.

It is a pleasing thought. But another, more significant one, away from Lochaber is this: when the referee blew the final whistle on the life of Gentle Johnny, the life he called a great game, he had put behind him the early taunts of 'foreigner' and 'Pole' and the bitterness of Barlinnie in the bad old days. He had earned his Green Beret. The engraving on the Commando memorial said it all: 'United We Conquer'. John Ramsay would have savoured that word: UNITED.

During his criminal career, Johnny Ramensky blew open a remarkable number of safes and was a menace to society, and for this he paid a high price. It is without doubt that Ramensky's life of crime, his astonishing escapes from Peterhead prison and his personal criminal code would have brought him a degree of notoriety during his lifetime. But it was his war service, his desire to serve his country and the remarkable escapades he undertook behind enemy lines and without care for his own safety that set Johnny Ramensky apart from other criminals and created a legend that will endure. Without the sins of his criminal career there could have been no wartime redemption. Sadly for Johnny, he simply could not give up the thrills and excitement of his work, but perhaps on that Highland hill looking out over lochs and forest and in the shadow of Ben Nevis and Aonach Mor there stands, for eternity, the real memorial to the man who wrote himself into history as Gentle Johnny.

# APPENDIX

## ANY PREVIOUS CONVICTIONS?
## YES, MY LORD . . .

1916   Glasgow Police Court. Theft. Admonished.

1921   Glasgow Police Court. Theft. Fined 10s/6d or seven days detention.

1921   Glasgow Sheriff Court. Theft. Three years borstal training.

1925   Edinburgh High Court. Theft by housebreaking with intent to steal. Attempted housebreaking with intent to steal. Assault. Eighteen months.

1927   Glasgow. Theft by housebreaking. Three years penal servitude.

1929   Glasgow Police Court. Known thief loitering with intent to steal. One year hard labour.

1929   Greenock Sheriff Court. Theft by housebreaking. Opening lockfast premises. Theft by housebreaking. Eighteen months imprisonment.

1934   Edinburgh High Court. Theft by housebreaking. Opening lockfast premises. Theft by housebreaking. Five years penal servitude.

1938   Aberdeen High Court. Theft by housebreaking. Opening lockfast premises. Five years penal servitude.

1947 York Assizes. Malicious damage and contravention of Larceny Act 1916, section 27. Five years on each offence to run concurrently.

1951 Glasgow High Court. Theft by housebreaking, opening lockfast premises. Five years imprisonment under section 22 of Criminal Justice (Scotland) Act 1949.

1955 Edinburgh High Court. Theft by housebreaking. Opening lockfast premises. Ten years.

1959 Aberdeen Sheriff Court. Absconding from legal custody and attempting to defeat the ends of justice. Eighteen months imprisonment (Edinburgh Appeal Court – sentence reduced to twelve months imprisonment).

1964 Paisley Sheriff Court. Housebreaking and attempted opening lockfast place with intent to steal. Two years.

1967 Glasgow High Court. Theft by housebreaking. Opening lockfast premises with intent to steal. Four years.

1970 Stirling Sheriff Court. Housebreaking and opening lockfast place with intent to steal. Housebreaking with intent to steal. Two years.

1972 Charged in Ayr under Prevention of Crime Act. One year.

# CATEGORY:
# HIGH RISK OF ESCAPE

John Ramsay a.k.a. John Ramenski a.k.a. John Ramensky a.k.a.
Yonus Ramanauckas

**Peterhead escapes:**

November 1934  –  twenty-nine hours at large.
August 1952      –  recaptured the following day.
February 1958    –  recaptured the following day.
October 1958     –  recaptured the following day.
December 1958   –  around nine days at large.

In five escapes he never managed to travel further than a few
dozen miles from the prison.

# INDEX